MY FACTFILE!

FILL IN YOUR FOOTY DETAILS!

MY NAME IS...

MY FAVOURITE FOOTBALL TEAM IS...

MY FAVOURITE PLAYER IS...

THE POSITION I PLAY IN IS...

THE TEAMS I PLAY FOR ARE...

MY FAVOURITE FOOTBALL BOOTS ARE...

MATCH!

FOOTBALL RECORDS BOOK!

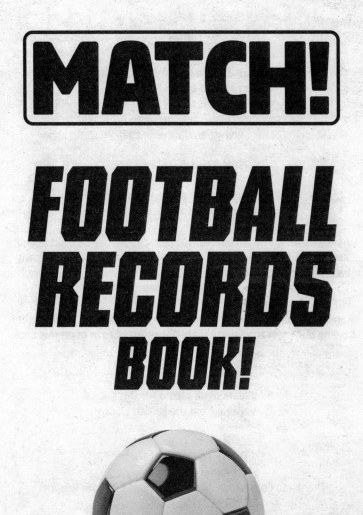

MACMILLAN CHILDREN'S BOOKS

First published 2019 by Macmillan Children's Books
an imprint of Pan Macmillan
The Smithson, 6 Briset Street, London, EC1M 5NR
Associated companies throughout the world
www.panmacmillan.com

ISBN 978-1-5290-2672-6

135798642

A CIP catalogue record for this book
is available from the British Library.

Written by Jared Tinslay
Designed by Darryl Tooth
Stats correct up to June 2019
Thanks to Calistemon and Abdelrhman 1990 for images.

Printed and bound by CPI Group (UK) Ltd, Croydon CR0 4YY

CONTENTS!

REST OF THE WORLD

WOMEN'S FOOTBALL

HALF-TIME

SECOND HALF

WORLD CUP

EUROPEAN CHAMPIONSHIP

ENGLAND

SCOTLAND

PREMIER LEAGUE

The Premier League was founded in 1992, replacing the old First Division!

LEAGUE WINNERS

MAN. UNITED ★ 13 TITLES

As well as being the first ever side to get their hands on the Premier League trophy back in the 1992-93 season, Man. United are also the club with the most titles to their name - a whopping 13! The Red Devils' most recent success came in 2012-13, when Robin van Persie netted 26 league goals to end the Prem campaign as top scorer - with rivals Man. City coming in second place!

FAB FACT!

United are one of just six teams to have contested every Premier League season!

 **DID YOU KNOW?**

Blackburn won the Prem trophy in 1994–95 by a single point – they just edged Man. United to win their first and only PL title!

CHAMPIONS - LAST 15 SEASONS

YEAR	CHAMPIONS	SECOND PLACE	THIRD PLACE	TOP SCORER
2018-19	**Man. City**	Liverpool	Chelsea	Mohamed Salah Sadio Mane PE. Aubameyang
2017-18	**Man. City**	Man. United	Tottenham	Mohamed Salah
2016-17	**Chelsea**	Tottenham	Man. City	Harry Kane
2015-16	**Leicester**	Arsenal	Tottenham	Harry Kane
2014-15	**Chelsea**	Man. City	Arsenal	Sergio Aguero
2013-14	**Man. City**	Liverpool	Chelsea	Luis Suarez
2012-13	**Man. United**	Man. City	Chelsea	Robin van Persie
2011-12	**Man. City**	Man. United	Arsenal	Robin van Persie
2010-11	**Man. United**	Chelsea	Man. City	Carlos Tevez Dimitar Berbatov
2009-10	**Chelsea**	Man. United	Arsenal	Didier Drogba
2008-09	**Man. United**	Liverpool	Chelsea	Nicolas Anelka
2007-08	**Man. United**	Chelsea	Arsenal	Cristiano Ronaldo
2006-07	**Man. United**	Chelsea	Liverpool	Didier Drogba
2005-06	**Chelsea**	Man. United	Liverpool	Thierry Henry
2004-05	**Chelsea**	Arsenal	Man. United	Thierry Henry

Alan Shearer

FAB FACT!

Nobody has scored more goals in one PL game than Shearer – he once hit five!

The undisputed Prem goal king is ex-Southampton, Blackburn and Newcastle striker **ALAN SHEARER**! He scored all his Premier League goals for Rovers and The Magpies, winning the title with the former and finishing his career as the latter's all-time top scorer. He won three PL Golden Boot awards, has scored more penalties than any other player and holds the joint-record for most hat-tricks. The current PL player with most goals is Man. City hero **SERGIO AGUERO**!

Sergio Aguero

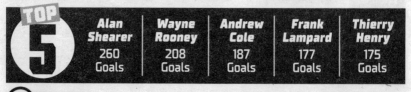

TOP 5	Alan Shearer	Wayne Rooney	Andrew Cole	Frank Lampard	Thierry Henry
	260 Goals	208 Goals	187 Goals	177 Goals	175 Goals

MOST APPEARANCES

GARETH BARRY ★ 653 GAMES

FAB FACT!
Barry played over half of his PL games for his first team Aston Villa!

Gareth Barry

The one player to make over 650 Premier League appearances only left the league at the end of 2017-18 – **GARETH BARRY**! The former England international midfielder featured for Aston Villa, Man. City, Everton and West Brom, and finally broke the appearances record when he was turning out for The Baggies against Arsenal in September 2017! However, since the Prem started tracking minutes played at the start of 2006-07, ex-GK **PETR CECH** tops the list!

Petr Cech

	Gareth Barry	Ryan Giggs	Frank Lampard	David James	Gary Speed
TOP 5	653 Games	632 Games	609 Games	572 Games	535 Games

CRAZY FACTS!

2

Two players have scored Premier League penalties with both feet – Bobby Zamora and Obafemi Martins!

11

Jamie Vardy holds the record for most consecutive games scored in – he busted net in 11 games in a row in 2015!

5

Five goalkeepers have a Prem goal – Peter Schmeichel, Brad Friedel, Paul Robinson, Tim Howard and Asmir Begovic!

2:56

Sadio Mane hit the quickest Prem hat-trick ever back in 2015 when playing for Southampton - he took just two minutes and 56 seconds!

41

Ex-footy manager Les Reed holds the record for shortest managerial reign - he was in charge of Charlton for just 41 days in 2006. Bonkers!

4

Lewis Dunk shares the unfortunate record of most own goals in a single PL season - he scored four in 2017-18!

STRANGE but true!

Darius Vassell

There have been some very odd Premier League injuries over the years, with ex-England GK **David James** once pulling a back muscle when he was reaching for the TV remote, but none more so than **Darius Vassell**'s. . . The ex-Aston Villa striker needed to have one of his toenails removed because it had got infected but, instead of seeking the help of club surgeons, he went in search of a DIY solution! He decided to use an electric drill at home to try to remove the nail himself but, unsurprisingly, made things quite a lot worse and missed his side's next three Prem matches. What a fail!

David James

EFL CHAMPIONSHIP

The EFL Championship, founded in 2004, is the highest division of the English Football League!

LEAGUE WINNERS

NEWCASTLE, READING, SUNDERLAND & WOLVES ★ 2 TITLES

There's not an outright leader for EFL Championship titles currently - instead, four teams have won the trophy twice! Newcastle, Reading, Sunderland and Wolves are the four clubs to have gone up to the Premier League as Championship winners on two occasions, although most teams would just take one of the two automatic promotion spots at the start of a new campaign!

FAB FACT!

Reading's massive tally of 106 points in 2005-06 is a record for the EFL Championship!

DID YOU KNOW?

In the first 15 seasons, seven of the play-off winners had finished third in the table in that particular campaign!

PROMOTED TEAMS - LAST 15 SEASONS

YEAR	CHAMPIONS	SECOND PLACE	PLAY-OFFS	TOP SCORER
2018-19	Norwich	Sheffield United	Aston Villa	Teemu Pukki
2017-18	Wolves	Cardiff	Fulham	Matej Vydra
2016-17	Newcastle	Brighton	Huddersfield	Chris Wood
2015-16	Burnley	Middlesbrough	Hull	Andre Gray
2014-15	Bournemouth	Watford	Norwich	Daryl Murphy
2013-14	Leicester	Burnley	QPR	Ross McCormack
2012-13	Cardiff	Hull	Crystal Palace	Glenn Murray
2011-12	Reading	Southampton	West Ham	Rickie Lambert
2010-11	QPR	Norwich	Swansea	Danny Graham
2009-10	Newcastle	West Brom	Blackpool	Peter Whittingham Nicky Maynard
2008-09	Wolves	Birmingham	Burnley	Sylvan Ebanks-Blake
2007-08	West Brom	Stoke	Hull	Sylvan Ebanks-Blake
2006-07	Sunderland	Birmingham	Derby	Jamie Cureton
2005-06	Reading	Sheffield United	Watford	Marlon King
2004-05	Sunderland	Wigan	West Ham	Nathan Ellington

TOP GOALSCORERS

DAVID NUGENT & ROSS McCORMACK ★ 120 GOALS

FAB FACT!
McCormack's transfer fees have totalled over £20 million throughout his career!

Help·Link

Ross McCormack

At the end of the 2018-19 season, **ROSS McCORMACK** and **DAVID NUGENT** were both dead level on 120 Championship goals each! The Scotland striker just had the edge in MATCH's eyes, though – he reached the landmark by playing 58 fewer matches and over 2,000 fewer minutes than his goal rival! McCormack also has a Championship Golden Boot to his name for when he was playing for Leeds – something that Nugent can't boast about either!

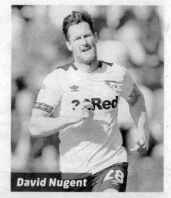

David Nugent

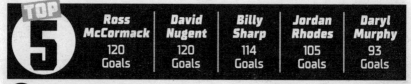

TOP 5	Ross McCormack	David Nugent	Billy Sharp	Jordan Rhodes	Daryl Murphy
	120 Goals	120 Goals	114 Goals	105 Goals	93 Goals

MOST APPEARANCES

LEE CAMP ★ 493 GAMES

FAB FACT!
Camp's played over 44,000 minutes of action in the Championship. EFL legend!

Lee Camp

He hasn't always been first choice at every team he's played for, but veteran goalkeeper **LEE CAMP** has still racked up more than 400 Championship appearances for eight different clubs – more than any other player! Centre-back **LUKE CHAMBERS** isn't too far behind, and holds the record for most games as an outfield player. Unlike Camp though, Chambers made it to 400 Champo games by playing for just two teams in his class career - Nottingham Forest and Ipswich!

Luke Chambers

TOP 5	Lee Camp	Luke Chambers	Cole Skuse	Chris Gunter	Richard Keogh
	493 Games	459 Games	429 Games	416 Games	409 Games

CRAZY FACTS!

11 The total attendance for every Championship game in 2018-19 was close to 11 million. Wow!

30,000

Sheffield Wednesday's Hillsborough Stadium holds nearly 30,000 more fans than Luton's Kenilworth Road!

10 No gaffer has won the Championship Manager Of The Month award more times than Neil Warnock!

23 Rotherham's shocking points tally of 23 in 2016-17 is the worst in Championship history!

46

Tom Ince's dad Paul also played in the Championship – 46 times for Wolves!

30

Glenn Murray's 30 Championship goals back in 2012-13 for Crystal Palace is a single-season best!

STRANGE but true!

Frank Lampard celebrates

It's normal for teams to do their homework on opponents – managers will sometimes even go to games to get a better glimpse of their tactics. It's not so normal to send spies to secretly watch opponents in training, but that didn't stop Leeds manager **Marcelo Bielsa** before their match against rivals **Derby** in January 2019! Unfortunately though for Bielsa, his spy was hardly James Bond – Rams staff spotted him lurking around and the police had to come to move him on! The Whites were fined £200,000, and still won the clash 2-0, but Frank Lampard's Derby had the last laugh by beating Bielsa's side in the play-offs!

Marcelo Bielsa

FA CUP

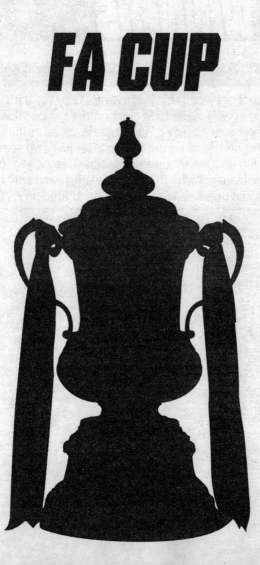

The FA Cup is the oldest national football competition in the world, with over 700 teams competing for the trophy!

CUP WINNERS

ARSENAL ★ 13 TITLES

The Gunners won their first ever FA Cup way back in 1930, but they really made their mark on the competition when Arsene Wenger took charge of the club! He joined as manager in 1996, and got his hands on the trophy after just two seasons. He went on to win another six during his incredible 22-year reign, and retired as the manager with most FA Cup titles – and with the north London club just one trophy ahead of Man. United on FA Cup wins!

WINNERS 2015

FAB FACT!
The Gunners have appeared in 20 different Finals – only United have contested as many!

DID YOU KNOW?

The 2001 to 2006 finals were held at Cardiff's Millennium Stadium while Wembley Stadium was undergoing redevelopment!

CHAMPIONS - LAST 15 SEASONS

YEAR	CHAMPIONS	RUNNERS-UP	RESULT	ATTENDANCE
2018-19	Man. City	Watford	6-0	85,854
2017-18	Chelsea	Man. United	1-0	87,647
2016-17	Arsenal	Chelsea	2-1	89,472
2015-16	Man. United	Crystal Palace	2-1 AET	88,619
2014-15	Arsenal	Aston Villa	4-0	89,283
2013-14	Arsenal	Hull	3-2 AET	89,345
2012-13	Wigan	Man. City	1-0	86,254
2011-12	Chelsea	Liverpool	2-1	89,102
2010-11	Man. City	Stoke	1-0	88,643
2009-10	Chelsea	Portsmouth	1-0	88,335
2008-09	Chelsea	Everton	2-1	89,391
2007-08	Portsmouth	Cardiff	1-0	89,874
2006-07	Chelsea	Man. United	1-0 AET	89,826
2005-06	Liverpool	West Ham	3-3 Liverpool won on pens	71,140
2004-05	Arsenal	Man. United	0-0 Arsenal won on pens	71,876

FINAL GOALS

IAN RUSH ★ 5 GOALS

FAB FACT!
Four of Rush's five FA Cup final goals came against The Reds' rivals Everton!

Ian Rush

Liverpool's all-time leading scorer **IAN RUSH** holds the record for most nets busted in FA Cup finals, while Chelsea striker **DIDIER DROGBA** scored in more individual finals than any other player - four! The ex-Blues targetman holds another interesting FA Cup record too... He's scored more match-winning final goals in the tournament than any other player - i.e. the ones that really count. And that's what our top five celebrates - players who hit FA Cup final deciders!

Didier Drogba

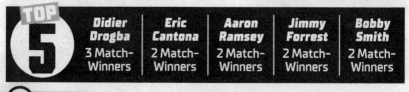

TOP 5	Didier Drogba	Eric Cantona	Aaron Ramsey	Jimmy Forrest	Bobby Smith
	3 Match-Winners	2 Match-Winners	2 Match-Winners	2 Match-Winners	2 Match-Winners

MOST TITLES

ASHLEY COLE ★ 7 TITLES

FAB FACT!
His first ever FA Cup Final for Arsenal was against his future club Chelsea!

Ashley Cole with Chelsea

With Arsenal having won so many FA Cup trophies under Wenger in the 21st century, it was always likely that the most decorated player in the tournament's history would be a Gunner – and it is! The thing about **ASHLEY COLE** though, is that the left-back actually lifted more FA Cup trophies after moving to Chelsea in 2006 – four of his seven medals came while he was wearing blue, while his other three were for the north Londoners. He's a total FA Cup legend!

Ashley Cole with Arsenal

TOP 5	Ashley Cole	Petr Cech	Patrick Vieira	Paul Scholes	Olivier Giroud
	7 Titles	5 Titles	5 Titles	4 Titles	4 Titles

CRAZY FACTS!

The first ever FA Cup final was played at the Kennington Oval, which is now a cricket ground!

1872

1

Only one team has ever won the cup and been relegated in the same season - Wigan in 2013!

26

The biggest ever victory recorded in the tourno was a huge 26-0 win for Preston over Hyde in 1887 - a real 'hyding'!

113

It took 113 years for the first ever red card in an FA Cup final - Man. United's Kevin Moran was sent off in 1985!

25

Ex-Everton striker Louis Saha scored the fastest ever FA Cup final goal - it took him just 25 seconds to net v Chelsea in 2009!

4

Leicester have reached more finals without lifting the famous cup than any other team!

STRANGE but true!

Derby v Charlton in 1946

When we talk about the FA Cup, one of the most common phrases is 'The magic of the cup'! Some strange things have happened over the years, such as non-league sides Sutton United and Lincoln making it to the Fifth Round in 2017, or League Two's **Bradford** beating Chelsea away in 2015. But another mystery happened in 1946. Derby were facing **Charlton** in the final, but the ball suddenly burst when their striker had a shot on goal! Then, a year later, Charlton made it to the final again - and the same thing happened! Was it dodgy balls or simply the magic of the cup?

Bradford celebrate v Chelsea

EFL CUP

The annual EFL Cup is open to any team competing in the top four levels of the English Football League system!

CUP WINNERS

LIVERPOOL ★ 8 TITLES

 The Reds last won the EFL Cup in 2012, but it was in the 80s that they really took charge of the cool competition! They won the title in four straight seasons – from 1981 to 1984 – and came second in 1987 as well! They're currently just ahead of Man. City in the battle to be the EFL Cup's top dogs, though – 2019 was the Manchester giant's fourth title in six years!

FAB FACT!

Liverpool have appeared in 12 different finals – more than any other club!

DID YOU KNOW?

From 1981 to 1986, the EFL Cup was actually known as the Milk Cup due to sponsorship reasons!

CHAMPIONS - LAST 15 SEASONS

YEAR	CHAMPIONS	RUNNERS-UP	RESULT	ATTENDANCE
2018-19	Man. City	Chelsea	0-0 City won on pens	81,775
2017-18	Man. City	Arsenal	3-0	85,671
2016-17	Man. United	Southampton	3-2	85,264
2015-16	Man. City	Liverpool	1-1 City won on pens	86,206
2014-15	Chelsea	Tottenham	2-0	89,294
2013-14	Man. City	Sunderland	3-1	84,697
2012-13	Swansea	Bradford	5-0	82,597
2011-12	Liverpool	Cardiff	2-2 Liverpool won on pens	89,041
2010-11	Birmingham	Arsenal	2-1	88,851
2009-10	Man. United	Aston Villa	2-1	88,596
2008-09	Man. United	Tottenham	0-0 United won on pens	88,217
2007-08	Tottenham	Chelsea	2-1 AET	87,660
2006-07	Chelsea	Arsenal	2-1	70,073
2005-06	Man. United	Wigan	4-0	66,866
2004-05	Chelsea	Liverpool	3-2 AET	78,000

FINAL GOALS

DIDIER DROGBA ★ 4 GOALS

FAB FACT!
Drogba was the first player to bust net in three different EFL Cup finals!

Didier Drogba

DIDIER DROGBA was certainly the man for the big occasions – and the scorer of important goals! He ended his career with three EFL Cup winners' medals for Chelsea, although perhaps his most important moment came in the 2006-07 final against Arsenal. The Ivory Coast striker scored a match-winning double as The Blues came from behind to beat their London rivals! **WAYNE ROONEY** also hit three EFL Cup final goals, including the winner against Aston Villa back in 2010!

Wayne Rooney

TOP 5

Didier Drogba	Wayne Rooney	Clive Clark	Ronnie Whelan	Michael Owen
4 Final Goals	3 Final Goals	3 Final Goals	3 Final Goals	2 Final Goals

MOST TITLES

IAN RUSH ★ 5 TITLES

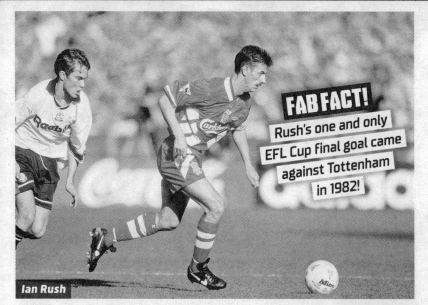

Ian Rush

FAB FACT!

Rush's one and only EFL Cup final goal came against Tottenham in 1982!

Lethal goal machine **IAN RUSH** was a key part of the incredible Liverpool side that won four straight EFL Cup titles in the early 80s! He left the club to join Juventus for a one-year spell in 1987, but returned to Merseyside in 1988 and ended up winning his fifth and final League Cup trophy in 1995! It's no surprise to see some **MAN. CITY** stars also in this list - they've dominated the tournament in recent seasons and could soon be catching up with the Reds hero!

Sergio Aguero

TOP 5	Ian Rush	Sergio Aguero	Vincent Kompany	David Silva	Wayne Rooney
	5 Titles	4 Titles	4 Titles	4 Titles	4 Titles

CRAZY FACTS!

Tottenham's Clive Allen scored 12 League Cup goals in 1986-87 – a single season record!

12

10

West Ham thrashed Bury 10-0 in the second round in 1983 – a joint-heaviest EFL Cup win. Wowzers!

32

It took 32 penalties for Derby to beat Carlisle in 2016 – their shootout finished 14-13. Woah!

20,000

The EFL Cup trophy is worth around £20,000!

2

No player's won more Man Of The Match awards in EFL Cup finals than Vincent Kompany!

Oldham's Frankie Bunn scored six net-busters in one match against Scarborough in 1989!

6

STRANGE but true!

Willy Caballero

One of the very first things you're told when you start playing footy is that you have to respect your manager's decisions! But, in the 2018-19 EFL Cup final between Chelsea and Man. City, Blues goalie **Kepa** seemed to have a total mind blank! His manager Maurizio Sarri wanted to replace him for Chelsea substitute keeper **Willy Caballero** in the final minutes of the match for the upcoming penalty shootout, but Kepa was having none of it! He point-blank refused to go off, even after CB David Luiz tried to convince him – much to his gaffer's annoyance! Then, after all the fiasco, he couldn't even help his side win the shootout!

Kepa

SCOTTISH PREMIERSHIP

The Scottish Premiership was founded in 2013, replacing the old Scottish Premier League!

LEAGUE WINNERS

CELTIC ★ 6 TITLES

Rangers may have won more all-time Scottish top-flight titles, but to say Celtic have dominated the Premiership era would be an understatement – The Bhoys have won every league title since its first season! It looked like there could be a real title battle in 2018-19 between themselves and The Gers, but they still finished nine points ahead of their Old Firm rivals!

FAB FACT!
The Hoops won the 2016–17 title by a massive 30 points, reaching 100+ points for the first time!

Ladbrokes
PREMIERSHIP

DID YOU KNOW?

The 2016–17 campaign was Rangers' first in the Scottish Premiership – they'd dropped to the Third Division in 2012 due to financial problems!

CHAMPIONS - LAST 15 SEASONS

YEAR	CHAMPIONS	SECOND PLACE	THIRD PLACE	TOP SCORER
2018-19	Celtic	Rangers	Kilmarnock	Alfredo Morelos
2017-18	Celtic	Aberdeen	Rangers	Kris Boyd
2016-17	Celtic	Aberdeen	Rangers	Liam Boyce
2015-16	Celtic	Aberdeen	Hearts	Leigh Griffiths
2014-15	Celtic	Aberdeen	Inverness CT	Adam Rooney
2013-14	Celtic	Motherwell	Aberdeen	Kris Commons
2012-13	Celtic	Motherwell	St. Johnstone	Michael Higdon
2011-12	Celtic	Rangers	Motherwell	Gary Hooper
2010-11	Rangers	Celtic	Hearts	Kenny Miller
2009-10	Rangers	Celtic	Dundee United	Kris Boyd
2008-09	Rangers	Celtic	Hearts	Kris Boyd
2007-08	Celtic	Rangers	Motherwell	Scott McDonald
2006-07	Celtic	Rangers	Aberdeen	Kris Boyd
2005-06	Celtic	Hearts	Rangers	Kris Boyd
2004-05	Rangers	Celtic	Hibernian	John Hartson

TOP GOALSCORERS

LEIGH GRIFFITHS ★ 75 GOALS

FAB FACT!
Griffiths also spent two seasons on loan at Hibs during the Scottish Premier League era. Class!

Leigh Griffiths

Celtic signed **LEIGH GRIFFITHS** from Wolves halfway through the 2013-14 season, and he went on to hit seven goals in 13 appearances in the second half of the season! His standout campaign was definitely 2015-16, though – he busted 31 Scottish Prem nets in 34 matches, winning the Golden Boot by ten goals! Ex-Aberdeen man **ADAM ROONEY** came third that season, and sits second in the all-time charts after scoring plenty in his five campaigns in the Premiership!

Adam Rooney

TOP 5	Leigh Griffiths	Adam Rooney	Kris Boyd	Kris Doolan	Liam Boyce
	75 Goals	65 Goals	53 Goals	52 Goals	48 Goals

FAB FACT!
Shinnie joined Aberdeen from Inverness CT, where he'd won the Scottish Cup in 2015!

Graeme Shinnie

Before joining Derby in July 2019, top-quality left-back slash central midfielder **GRAEME SHINNIE** was the captain of Aberdeen! He was given the armband in the summer of 2017, and led his team to a second-placed finish the following season - nine points behind champions Celtic! Shinnie is likely to be overtaken at the top of the charts soon, though - **DAVID WOTHERSPOON**'s not far behind him, and the midfielder is still playing in the Prem for St. Johnstone...

David Wotherspoon

TOP 5

Graeme Shinnie	David Wotherspoon	Paul McGowan	Steven Lawless	Andy Considine
217 Games	204 Games	196 Games	192 Games	191 Games

CRAZY FACTS!

Celtic's Jack Aitchison became the league's youngest scorer in May 2016 – he was just 16 when he scored v Motherwell!

16

0

Celtic went the whole of the 2016-17 campaign without suffering defeat!

19

The £19.7 million fee Celtic received from Lyon in 2018 for Moussa Dembele was a Scottish Premiership record!

2 Aberdeen's Sam Cosgrove is one of two players to be given a straight red card on their Scottish Prem debut!

10 Kilmarnock's Kris Boyd scored after just 10 seconds against Ross County in January 2017!

4 In 2018-19, Rangers were awarded four penalties in a match against St. Mirren!

STRANGE but true!

Ross McRorie

When Rangers played Hibs in May 2019, Gers manager **Steven Gerrard** was faced with a manager's worst nightmare. . . He'd made all three subs going into the last moments of the game, before his goalkeeper decided to kick an opponent and get sent off! The ex-Liverpool CM decided that midfielder **Ross McRorie** would be his best option to take the gloves, despite the player admitting on Rangers TV a few months earlier that he was "hopeless" in goal! It didn't turn out too badly for Ross, whose brother is actually a professional GK, as he kept a clean sheet and his side won 1-0!

Steven Gerrard

LA LIGA

Spain's top competition was founded way back in 1929, and originally there were only ten teams in the division!

LEAGUE WINNERS

REAL MADRID ★ 33 TITLES

🏆 There's a reason why Real Madrid were top of the planet's footy rich list in 2019, and with tons more fans on Facebook, Twitter and Instagram than any other club – they've been super successful over the last century! Even though rivals Barcelona have made up some ground in the last decade, supporters of Los Blancos will remind them that they're still behind in the all-time league titles list!

FAB FACT!

The 121 goals Real scored on their way to the 2011-12 La Liga title is an all-time record!

DID YOU KNOW?

Of the founding La Liga sides, only Real Madrid, Barcelona and Athletic Bilbao have NEVER suffered relegation!

CHAMPIONS - LAST 15 SEASONS

YEAR	CHAMPIONS	SECOND PLACE	THIRD PLACE	TOP SCORER
2018-19	Barcelona	Atletico Madrid	Real Madrid	Lionel Messi
2017-18	Barcelona	Atletico Madrid	Real Madrid	Lionel Messi
2016-17	Real Madrid	Barcelona	Atletico Madrid	Lionel Messi
2015-16	Barcelona	Real Madrid	Atletico Madrid	Luis Suarez
2014-15	Barcelona	Real Madrid	Atletico Madrid	Cristiano Ronaldo
2013-14	Atletico Madrid	Barcelona	Real Madrid	Cristiano Ronaldo
2012-13	Barcelona	Real Madrid	Atletico Madrid	Lionel Messi
2011-12	Real Madrid	Barcelona	Valencia	Lionel Messi
2010-11	Barcelona	Real Madrid	Valencia	Cristiano Ronaldo
2009-10	Barcelona	Real Madrid	Valencia	Lionel Messi
2008-09	Barcelona	Real Madrid	Sevilla	Diego Forlan
2007-08	Real Madrid	Villarreal	Barcelona	Daniel Guiza
2006-07	Real Madrid	Barcelona	Sevilla	Ruud van Nistelrooy
2005-06	Barcelona	Real Madrid	Valencia	Samuel Eto'o
2004-05	Barcelona	Real Madrid	Villarreal	Diego Forlan

FAB FACT!

As well as being La Liga's all-time top scorer, Leo's also got more assists than any other player!

Lionel Messi

We'd need another book just to go through all the goal records that **LEO MESSI**'s smashed in his incredible Barcelona career! He was the first player to reach the 300-goal milestone, and might be the only ever hero to reach 400+ La Liga goals. His jaw-dropping 2011-12 season was his personal best, though – he somehow busted 50 nets in 37 games, which is the best single-season tally ever – just ahead of rival **CRISTIANO RONALDO**'s 48 in 2014-15!

Cristiano Ronaldo

TOP 5	Lionel Messi	Cristiano Ronaldo	Telmo Zarra	Hugo Sanchez	Raul Gonzalez
	419 Goals	311 Goals	251 Goals	234 Goals	228 Goals

MOST APPEARANCES

ANDONI ZUBIZARRETA ★ 622 GAMES

FAB FACT!
He was also the most-capped player for Spain's national team for a number of years!

Andoni Zubizarreta

Ex-Athletic Bilbao and Barcelona keeper **ANDONI ZUBIZARRETA** is a real legend of Spanish footy - not just for making so many appearances! He spent five seasons with Bilbao, winning two La Liga titles and the Copa del Rey, before moving to La Blaugrana and bagging another four league trophies plus another two Copa del Rey medals - and the European Cup! Lethal Real Madrid striker **RAUL** is the only other superstar to make it to 550 matches!

Raul

TOP 5	Andoni Zubizarreta	Raul Gonzalez	Eusebio Sacristan	Francisco Buyo	Manolo Sanchis
	622 Games	550 Games	543 Games	542 Games	523 Games

CRAZY FACTS!

48

Ex-Real Sociedad player / manager Harry Lowe became the oldest La Liga player ever when he stepped on to the pitch in 1935 aged 48 years old!

6

There's a crown with 'Penalty King' and Diego Alves' name on it! The ex-Valencia GK saved six in 2016-17!

Barcelona's heated clash with rivals Espanyol in 2003 holds the record for most red cards - there were six in one match!

2003

43

Barcelona hold the record for the longest unbeaten run, when they went 43 league games without a loss from April 2017 to May 2018!

Cristiano Ronaldo has scored more La Liga penalties than any other player. Hero!

61

Catalan club Lleida hold the sorry record for most goals conceded in one season - a whoppin' 134!

134

STRANGE but true!

Luis Figo takes a corner for Real

When two of the planet's greatest rivals face off, tensions understandably run high, but one El Clasico in particular really got heated. . . **Luis Figo** had made a name for himself at **Barcelona** for being one of the best widemen around, so his move to **Real Madrid** in 2000 didn't please Los Cules one bit - and when he returned to the Nou Camp for the first time in a Real shirt, things really got out of hand. As well as having to face banners and constant jeers from Barça supporters, one fan even decided to throw a pig's head onto the pitch in protest, when the Portugal winger was taking a corner! Figo still had the last laugh - Los Galacticos won the title that year!

SERIE A

The Italian league boasts some of
the most famous and successful clubs
in the history of the game. . .

LEAGUE WINNERS

JUVENTUS ⭐ 35 TITLES

Italian powerhouse Juventus set an incredible new record in 2018-19 – they became the first ever side in Europe's top five leagues to win eight consecutive league titles! Their brutal dominance over the last decade has really extended their lead at the top of the all-time rankings – they've now won 17 more league titles than AC Milan and Inter, who are joint second in the charts!

FAB FACT!

Their massive 102 points tally in the 2013–14 season is a Serie A record!

DID YOU KNOW?

Juventus finished top of the Serie A table in 2004–05, but were stripped of their title because they were found guilty of match fixing!

CHAMPIONS - LAST 15 SEASONS

YEAR	CHAMPIONS	SECOND PLACE	THIRD PLACE	TOP SCORER
2018-19	Juventus	Napoli	Atalanta	Fabio Quagliarella
2017-18	Juventus	Napoli	Roma	Mauro Icardi Ciro Immobile
2016-17	Juventus	Roma	Napoli	Edin Dzeko
2015-16	Juventus	Napoli	Roma	Gonzalo Higuain
2014-15	Juventus	Roma	Lazio	Mauro Icardi Luca Toni
2013-14	Juventus	Roma	Napoli	Ciro Immobile
2012-13	Juventus	Napoli	AC Milan	Edinson Cavani
2011-12	Juventus	AC Milan	Udinese	Zlatan Ibrahimovic
2010-11	AC Milan	Inter	Napoli	Antonio di Natale
2009-10	Inter	Roma	AC Milan	Antonio di Natale
2008-09	Inter	Juventus	AC Milan	Zlatan Ibrahimovic
2007-08	Inter	Roma	Juventus	Alessandro Del Piero
2006-07	Inter	Roma	Lazio	Francesco Totti
2005-06	Inter	Roma	AC Milan	Luca Toni
2004-05	N/A	AC Milan	Inter	Cristiano Lucarelli

TOP GOALSCORERS

SILVIO PIOLA ★ 274 GOALS

FAB FACT!
Totti won Serie A's Player Of The Year award a record five times during his wicked 25-year career!

Francesco Totti

Italian Football Hall Of Fame hero **SILVIO PIOLA** is a national icon! As well as being the only player to have the honour of being all-time Serie A top scorer for three different teams - Pro Vercelli, Lazio and Novara - he also netted two goals in the 1938 World Cup final to help his nation lift the famous trophy! Not far behind him in the charts is another total Serie A legend - Roma ace **FRANCESCO TOTTI**, who holds the record for the most goals scored in Serie A for a single club!

Silvio Piola (Right)

	Silvio Piola	Francesco Totti	Gunnar Nordahl	Giuseppe Meazza	Jose Altafini
TOP 5	274 Goals	250 Goals	225 Goals	216 Goals	216 Goals

MOST APPEARANCES

FAB FACT!
When Maldini retired in 2009, AC retired their number three shirt with him!

Paolo Maldini

Just like Totti, **PAOLO MALDINI** spent his whole career at just one club – AC Milan! The versatile defender, who could play left-back or centre-back, won 26 trophies for The Red and Blacks and was their captain for a number of years too! Top-class keeper **GIANLUIGI BUFFON** came really close to reaching Maldini's record before he left to join PSG, but now he's back at Juventus he should top this list very soon. The ace goalkeeper is an all-time Serie A legend!

Gianluigi Buffon

TOP 5

Paolo Maldini	Gianluigi Buffon	Francesco Totti	Javier Zanetti	Gianluca Pagliuca
647 Games	640 Games	619 Games	615 Games	592 Games

CRAZY FACTS!

By winning Serie A with Juventus, Cristiano Ronaldo became the first player to win league titles in Italy, Spain and England. Class!

1

2000

In 2016, Juventus' Moise Kean became the first star born in the 2000s to play in one of Europe's five major leagues!

28

No player's scored more Serie A free-kicks than dead-ball demon and perfect passer Andrea Pirlo!

36 Gonzalo Higuain's 36 goals for Napoli in 2015-16 is the record for most goals in a single season!

39 Most players make their league debuts as teenagers, but Empoli GK Maurizio Pugliesi was 39 when he made his Serie A debut!

38 Juventus are the only team to have gone an entire 38-game season without losing - they did it back in 2011-12!

STRANGE but true!

Buffon saves a penalty

Legendary shot-stopper **Gianluigi Buffon** has been around for a very long time! In fact, he said he was almost ready to retire back in 2016 after Fiorentina wonderkid Federico Chiesa made his Serie A debut against him! It wasn't that the wicked winger was too quick or deadly at shooting, it was that Gigi had actually played with Federico's dad Enrico at Parma back in the late 1990s – and it made him feel old! After joining PSG, he also came up against his former Juve and Parma team-mate Lilian Thuram's son Marcus – they even swapped shirts post-game to mark the moment!

Marcus Thuram and Buffon

EURO LEAGUES

BUNDESLIGA

LIGUE 1
Conforama

eredivisie

LIGA NOS

This section takes a closer look at the German, French, Dutch and Portuguese leagues!

GERMANY

FAB FACT!
The four stars above Bayern's badge represent all their Bundesliga title wins!

FUSSBALLMEISTER 2019

BUNDESLIGA

FC BAYERN MÜNCHEN

Bayern Munich

They won just four of the first 16 Bundesliga titles, but **BAYERN MUNICH** have dominated the German league in recent years! The 2018-19 trophy was their seventh on the spin, and edged them closer to the incredible 30 milestone. They just pipped **BORUSSIA DORTMUND** to the title on the final day, and the Black and Yellows were actually the last team to win the league apart from Bayern - they lifted the cool trophy consecutively in 2010-11 and 2011-12!

Borrusia Dortmund

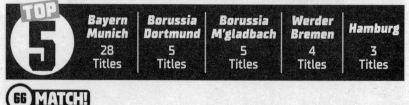

TOP 5

Bayern Munich	Borussia Dortmund	Borussia M'gladbach	Werder Bremen	Hamburg
28 Titles	5 Titles	5 Titles	4 Titles	3 Titles

FAB FACT!

PSG's 96 points in the 2015-16 season is a Ligue 1 record!

PSG

🏆 The first ever professional French league was founded in 1932, but it was re-named, expanded to 20 clubs and born as Ligue 1 in 2002! **LYON** lifted the first six Ligue 1 titles (but haven't won it since), while **PSG** have totally dominated over the last decade. The mega rich club from the French capital won their sixth title in seven seasons in 2018-19, with Monaco the only team able to stop their dominance in 2016-17 – it was the Red and Whites first and only Ligue 1 trophy!

Monaco

	PSG	Lyon	Monaco	Lille	Marseille
TOP 5	6 Titles	6 Titles	1 Title	1 Title	1 Title

HOLLAND

AJAX ★ 26 EREDIVISIE TITLES

2018

KAMPIOEN EREDIVISIE

Ajax

FAB FACT!

Ajax are the only Dutch team to have won the Champions League!

The first Eredivisie season, in 1956-57, was won by **AJAX** – and they're the most successful Dutch club in history! They had a really memorable season in 2018-19, securing their first domestic double in 17 years by winning both the Dutch league and cup – plus reaching the Champions League semi-final! Ajax, their 'De Klassieker' rivals **FEYENOORD** and **PSV** are known as the 'Big Three' – the only sides to have appeared in every Eredivisie season!

PSV

TOP 5	Ajax	PSV	Feyenoord	AZ Alkmaar	Willem II
	26 Titles	21 Titles	10 Titles	2 Titles	1 Title

FAB FACT!
All Portuguese champions have either come from Lisbon or Porto!

Benfica

Just like in Holland, the Portuguese league has been totally dominated by three teams – **BENFICA**, **PORTO** and **SPORTING**! Between them, they've won all but two titles since the league was first founded in 1934, although Benfica have a decent lead at the top. The Eagles set a new record points tally in 2015-16 – they achieved 88 over the season, only recently matched by Porto in 2017-18! Porto and Benfica are the only two sides to have gone two seasons unbeaten, too!

Porto

TOP 5	Benfica	Porto	Sporting	Belenenses	Boavista
	37 Titles	28 Titles	18 Titles	1 Title	1 Title

CRAZY FACTS!

Saint-Etienne conceded just four Ligue 1 goals at home in 2007-08 – the best ever defensive home record!

4

9

PSG's 9-0 victory over Guingamp in January 2019 equalled the club's best Ligue 1 victory!

200+

Robert Lewandowski is the highest-scoring foreign player in Bundesliga history!

329

Nobody's played more Eredivisie matches than defender Pascal Bosschaart without scoring a goal!

9

No player has won more Bundesliga titles than winger Franck Ribery!

46

Ex-Sporting striker Hector Yazalde scored 46 league goals in 1973-74, winning the European Golden Shoe!

STRANGE but true!

Tony Chapron

Former Ligue 1 referee **Tony Chapron** handed out over 60 red cards during his time in France, but he should've given himself one during **Nantes**' match with **PSG** in January 2018! The official was running towards goal to cover a PSG attack, before being accidentally tripped over by Nantes' Diego Carlos who was running behind him. The referee didn't react well at all to the coming together – he actually kicked out at Carlos, then somehow decided to give him a red card! He apologised after the match, but still faced a six-month ban for his crazy actions!

TRANSFERS

This section checks out the richest clubs in the world and the planet's most expensive transfers!

MONEY CLUB

REAL MADRID ★ £665 MILLION PROFIT IN 2019

🏆 The Deloitte Football Money League ranks footy teams on a yearly basis depending on how much money they generate - and Real Madrid were top of the list at the start of 2019! Winning their third consecutive Champions League trophy in 2018 certainly would've helped, but the Spanish giants are always near the top of this particular table - they're easily one of the most-followed and successful sides in the world, and have been for absolutely ages!

FAB FACT!
No team has appeared in the top ten more times than Real Madrid – 16 times!

 74 MATCH!

DID YOU KNOW?

The Deloitte Football Money League first started ranking teams by their yearly profit back in 1997–98!

RICHEST CLUBS - LAST 15 YEARS

YEAR	FIRST PLACE	SECOND PLACE	THIRD PLACE	FOURTH PLACE
2019	Real Madrid	Barcelona	Man. United	Bayern Munich
2018	Man. United	Real Madrid	Barcelona	Bayern Munich
2017	Man. United	Barcelona	Real Madrid	Bayern Munich
2016	Real Madrid	Barcelona	Man. United	PSG
2015	Real Madrid	Man. United	Bayern Munich	Barcelona
2014	Real Madrid	Barcelona	Bayern Munich	Man. United
2013	Real Madrid	Barcelona	Man. United	Bayern Munich
2012	Real Madrid	Barcelona	Man. United	Bayern Munich
2011	Real Madrid	Barcelona	Man. United	Bayern Munich
2010	Real Madrid	Barcelona	Man. United	Bayern Munich
2009	Real Madrid	Man. United	Barcelona	Bayern Munich
2008	Real Madrid	Man. United	Barcelona	Chelsea
2007	Real Madrid	Barcelona	Juventus	Man. United
2006	Real Madrid	Man. United	AC Milan	Juventus
2005	Man. United	Real Madrid	AC Milan	Chelsea

RECORD OUTFIELDER

FAB FACT!
He made his pro debut for First club Santos when he was just 17 years old!

Neymar

When a 21-year-old **NEYMAR** joined Barcelona from Santos in 2013 for £48.6 million, it seemed a lot for a young talent that had never played in Europe, but the Spanish giants still managed to make a huge profit on him! La Blaugrana sold him to PSG four years later for close to £200 million, smashing the old world transfer record! In the same month, PSG captured **KYLIAN MBAPPE** on loan, but made him the most expensive teen when they signed him permanently in 2018!

Kylian Mbappe

	Neymar Jr.	Kylian Mbappe	Joao Felix	Antoine Griezmann	Philippe Coutinho
TOP 5	£198 million	£116 million	£113 million	£107 million	£106 million

RECORD GOALKEEPER

KEPA ARRIZABALAGA ★ £71 MILLION ★ 2018

FAB FACT!
Kepa kept 14 clean sheets in his debut Prem season in 2018-19!

Kepa

After just two seasons in Athletic Bilbao's first-team, Chelsea decided that **KEPA ARRIZABALAGA** was worth spending a lot of money on! They paid his buyout clause in full, making the Spanish goalkeeper the most-expensive player in his position! Liverpool keeper **ALISSON** was very briefly the most expensive GK in the world, too – he moved to The Reds for a world-record fee just under a month before Kepa joined the PL, and kept more clean sheets in his debut year than Kepa!

Alisson

TOP 5	Kepa Arrizabalaga	Alisson Becker	Ederson Moraes	Gianluigi Buffon	Thibaut Courtois
	£71 million	£65 million	£35 million	£32.6 million	£31.5 million

CRAZY FACTS!

Gareth Bale's £85 million deal to Real Madrid in 2013 made him the most expensive star from the UK in footy history!

85

75

Norwegian club Floey signed striker Kenneth Kristensen from rivals Vindbjart for 75kg of shrimp - it was how much the player weighed. LOL!

15 Romanian club UT Arad accepted a bid of 15kg of sausages for their defender Marius Cioara!

75

Virgil van Dijk became the world's most expensive defender, after costing Liverpool £75 million!

100

Willie Groves was the first ever player to cost £100, when he moved to Aston Villa back in 1893!

1975

In 1975, Giuseppe Savoldi signed for Napoli to become the first ever player to cost more than £1 million!

STRANGE but true!

Lewandowski at Poznan

Robert Lewandowski is still one of the most feared strikers in Europe, and one of the all-time top Bundesliga strikers, but his career could've been so different! In 2010, when he was still playing for Polish team Lech Poznan, he was offered the opportunity to sign for English club **Blackburn**! He was really tempted, but wanted to go to their training ground first and meet manager Sam Allardyce. Unfortunately for him, but more so for Rovers, an Icelandic volcano erupted and meant that his flight to England was cancelled because of ash clouds! He ended up staying in Poland and signing for Bayern Munich two months later!

CHAMPIONS LEAGUE

The Champions League is Europe's elite competition, replacing the European Cup in 1992!

CUP WINNERS

REAL MADRID ★ 7 TITLES

Three back-to-back trophies in 2016, 2017 and 2018 helped make Real Madrid the most successful club in Champo League history! They're three titles ahead of second-placed Barcelona, who last won the trophy in 2015. The two El Clasico giants' combined 11 titles make Spain the most successful country too, with English and Italian teams joint-second with five combined trophies each!

FAB FACT!

Real Madrid are the only team to win three consecutive Champions League titles!

DID YOU KNOW?

The first ever Champo League trophy was lifted by French club Marseille in 1993 – they haven't reached a CL final since!

CHAMPIONS - LAST 15 SEASONS

YEAR	CHAMPIONS	RUNNERS-UP	RESULT	ATTENDANCE
2018-19	Liverpool	Tottenham	2-0	63,272
2017-18	Real Madrid	Liverpool	3-1	61,561
2016-17	Real Madrid	Juventus	4-1	65,842
2015-16	Real Madrid	Atletico Madrid	1-1 Real won on pens	71,942
2014-15	Barcelona	Juventus	3-1	70,442
2013-14	Real Madrid	Atletico Madrid	4-1 AET	60,976
2012-13	Bayern Munich	B. Dortmund	2-1	86,298
2011-12	Chelsea	Bayern Munich	1-1 Chelsea won on pens	62,500
2010-11	Barcelona	Man. United	3-1	87,695
2009-10	Inter	Bayern Munich	2-0	73,490
2008-09	Barcelona	Man. United	2-0	62,467
2007-08	Man. United	Chelsea	1-1 United won on pens	67,310
2006-07	AC Milan	Liverpool	2-1	63,000
2005-06	Barcelona	Arsenal	2-1	79,610
2004-05	Liverpool	AC Milan	3-3 Liverpool won on pens	69,000

MATCH! 83

CRISTIANO RONALDO ★ 126 GOALS

FAB FACT!
Cristiano has scored four goals in five CL finals – more than any other player!

Cristiano Ronaldo

The king of the Champions League, **CRISTIANO RONALDO** was the competition's top scorer in six straight seasons for Real Madrid between 2012 and 2018, although he shared the prize with Neymar and Leo Messi in 2015. He was also top goalscorer in 2007-08 for Man. United! His 17 goals in the 2013-14 campaign was an all-time best for a single CL season, and he shares another scoring record with his footy rival **LIONEL MESSI** – they've both netted eight CL hat-tricks!

Lionel Messi

TOP 5

Cristiano Ronaldo	Lionel Messi	Raul Gonzalez	Karim Benzema	Ruud van Nistelrooy
126 Goals	112 Goals	71 Goals	60 Goals	56 Goals

MOST APPEARANCES

IKER CASILLAS ★ 177 GAMES

FAB FACT!
Casillas is the youngest GK to win the comp – he was 19 when Real won in 2000!

Iker Casillas

Legendary Spanish goalkeeper **IKER CASILLAS** featured in 20 consecutive Champo League campaigns for Real Madrid and Porto – and reached the knockout stage 19 times! He's saved more CL penalty kicks than any other player, holds the record for most clean sheets and is one of just two players to have won over 100 Champions League matches – a record he shares with old Real team-mate **CRISTIANO RONALDO**. Not a bad career for the legend GK, then!

Cristiano Ronaldo

TOP 5	Iker Casillas	Cristiano Ronaldo	Xavi Hernandez	Raul Gonzalez	Ryan Giggs
	177 Games	162 Games	151 Games	142 Games	141 Games

CRAZY FACTS!

6

Zlatan Ibrahimovic is the only player to have scored for six different teams!

38

Francesco Totti became the oldest player to score in the comp when he netted for Roma in 2014, aged 38!

69

Real Sociedad's Inigo Martinez scored the quickest own goal in CL history – it came after 69 seconds v Man. United in 2013!

23

The fastest penalty to be awarded in CL history was to Liverpool in the 2019 final against Spurs, after just 23 seconds!

3

Clarence Seedorf is the only hero to have won the trophy with three different teams – Ajax, Real Madrid and AC Milan!

9

James Milner's nine assists in 2017-18 set a single-season assists record!

MATCH! **87**

STRANGE but true!

The goal collapses in Madrid

We often refer to lethal strikers as 'net-busters', but before **Real Madrid**'s Champions League clash with **Borussia Dortmund** in April 1998, it was fans who broke the net! Both sets of players had entered the pitch, and were lining up for the anthem, when a group of Real 'Ultras' climbed onto the fence behind the goal. They pulled on the strings that were attached to the posts to keep them upright - forcing the goal to collapse on itself! There were no spare goalposts inside the ground, so the game was delayed for over an hour as Real officials had to travel to their training camp for more!

EUROPA LEAGUE

Europe's second biggest tourno changed format to become the Europa League in 2009!

CUP WINNERS

SEVILLA & ATLETICO MADRID ★ 3 TITLES

There's no separating La Liga's Sevilla and Atletico Madrid – they've both won three Europa League titles each! Atletico won the first ever edition of the competition in 2010, but Sevilla then won three in a row from 2014 to 2016! Unai Emery is therefore the most successful boss in the history of the tournament – he took Sevilla to their three Europa League trophies!

FAB FACT!

Atleti's 33 goals in the 2011–12 tourno is the third-highest in a single season!

 90 MATCH!

Before the 2009–10 season, the competition was called the UEFA Cup and had a different structure with fewer groups!

CHAMPIONS - LAST 15 SEASONS

YEAR	CHAMPIONS	RUNNERS-UP	RESULT	ATTENDANCE
2018-19	Chelsea	Arsenal	4-1	51,370
2017-18	Atletico Madrid	Marseille	3-0	55,768
2016-17	Man. United	Ajax	2-0	46,961
2015-16	Sevilla	Liverpool	3-1	34,429
2014-15	Sevilla	Dnipro	3-2	45,000
2013-14	Sevilla	Benfica	0-0 Sevilla won on pens	33,120
2012-13	Chelsea	Benfica	2-1	46,163
2011-12	Atletico Madrid	Athletic Bilbao	3-0	52,347
2010-11	Porto	Braga	1-0	45,391
2009-10	Atletico Madrid	Fulham	2-1 AET	49,000
2008-09	Shakhtar Donetsk	Werder Bremen	2-1 AET	37,357
2007-08	Zenit Saint Petersburg	Rangers	2-0	43,878
2006-07	Sevilla	Espanyol	2-2 Sevilla won on pens	50,670
2005-06	Sevilla	Middlesbrough	4-0	36,500
2004-05	CSKA Moscow	Sporting	3-1	47,085

RADAMEL FALCAO ★ 30 GOALS

FAB FACT!
He's scored three Europa League trebles – more than anyone else. Deadly!

Radamel Falcao

Known as 'The King of the Europa League', **RADAMEL FALCAO** won back-to-back tournos in 2011 and 2012 – for two different teams! He scored the winner in the final for Porto in 2011, ending the campaign with 17 goals and the top scorer prize, then did the same in 2011-12 – he bagged a brace in the final for Atletico and won the Golden Boot with 12 goals! **ARITZ ADURIZ** has never lifted the trophy, but was top scorer in 2015-16 and joint top in 2017-18 too!

Aritz Aduriz

TOP 5	Radamel Falcao	Aritz Aduriz	Kevin Gameiro	Oscar Cardozo	Alexandre Lacazette
	30 Goals	26 Goals	22 Goals	20 Goals	17 Goals

MOST APPEARANCES

DANIEL CARRICO ★ 60 GAMES

FAB FACT!
Carrico's scored one Europa League goal for Sevilla – in 2015 v Fiorentina!

Daniel Carrico

Rock-solid defender and defensive midfielder **DANIEL CARRICO** spent most of his early professional career with Sporting, where he played 26 times in the Europa League. He's enjoyed more success with Sevilla, though – he was in the starting line-up for all three of the club's trophy-winning finals! **GONZALO HIGUAIN** is just a couple of games behind Carrico, with Chelsea the third club he's turned out for in the tourno alongside two Serie A sides Napoli and AC Milan!

Gonzalo Higuain

TOP 5	Daniel Carrico	Gonzalo Higuain	Andreas Ulmer	Jeremain Lens	Senad Lulic
	60 Games	58 Games	55 Games	53 Games	52 Games

CRAZY FACTS!

17
Seventeen different German teams have taken part in the awesome tournament – more than any nation!

13
Sporting have been given 13 red cards in total in the comp – more than any club!

5
Valencia scored five first-half goals in the 2016 knockout clash against Rapid Vienna!

80,000

Spurs' clash with Gent in 2017 set a new Europa League attendance record – over 80,000 watched the game at Wembley!

16

Romelu Lukaku is the tournament's youngest scorer, netting when he was 16 for Anderlecht in 2009!

42

Ex-Tottenham GK Brad Friedel is the oldest player to appear in the comp – he was 42 when he turned out back in 2013!

STRANGE but true!

Fulham's Zoltan Gera celebrates

Fulham may be playing Championship footy in 2019-20, but not too long ago they were giant killing in Europe! In the very first edition of the tournament, a Cottagers team with the likes of Chris Baird, Bobby Zamora, Zoltan Gera, Chris Smalling, plus Roy Hodgson as manager, faced Italian titans Juventus in the last 16, after finishing second in their group and beating Shakhtar Donetsk in the previous round. It looked like their campaign was over after the Serie A side beat them 3-1 at home, but Fulham pulled of an epic comeback in the second leg and beat the megaclub 4-1 at Craven Cottage! They then made it all the way to the final, beating Wolfsburg and Hamburg along the way, but lost to Atletico Madrid in extra-time after an epic European run!

MLS

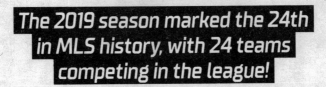

The 2019 season marked the 24th in MLS history, with 24 teams competing in the league!

TITLE WINNERS

LA GALAXY ★ 5 MLS CUPS

The MLS is split into the Western and Eastern Conferences, with teams then entering a play-off to land the prestigious MLS Cup! LA Galaxy are the team to have bagged the most MLS Cups – most recently in 2014, when ex-Republic Of Ireland forward Robbie Keane scored the winner in the final against New England Revolution. Wayne Rooney's DC United are hot on their heels, though – they're just one MLS Cup behind the superstars from Los Angeles!

FAB FACT!
LA Galaxy are one of the original eight teams to have participated in every MLS season!

CHAMPIONS

DID YOU KNOW?

The Supporters' Shield is awarded to the team with most points from both the Eastern and Western conferences!

CHAMPIONS - LAST 15 SEASONS

YEAR	CHAMPIONS	RUNNER-UP	SUPPORTERS' SHIELD	TOP SCORER
2018	Atlanta United	Portland Timbers	New York Red Bulls	Josef Martinez
2017	Toronto	Seattle Sounders	Toronto	Nemanja Nikolic
2016	Seattle Sounders	Toronto	FC Dallas	Bradley Wright-Phillips
2015	Portland Timbers	Columbus Crew	New York Red Bulls	Sebastian Giovinco Kei Kamara
2014	LA Galaxy	New England Revolution	Seattle Sounders	Bradley Wright-Phillips
2013	Sporting KC	Real Salt Lake	New York Red Bulls	Camilo Sanvezzo
2012	LA Galaxy	Houston Dynamo	San Jose Earthquakes	Chris Wondolowski
2011	LA Galaxy	Houston Dynamo	LA Galaxy	Dwayne de Rosario Chris Wondolowski
2010	Colorado Rapids	FC Dallas	LA Galaxy	Chris Wondolowski
2009	Real Salt Lake	LA Galaxy	Columbus Crew	Jeff Cunningham
2008	Columbus Crew	New York Red Bulls	Columbus Crew	Landon Donovan
2007	Houston Dynamo	New England Revolution	DC United	Luciano Emilio
2006	Houston Dynamo	New England Revolution	DC United	Jeff Cunningham
2005	LA Galaxy	New England Revolution	San Jose Earthquakes	Taylor Twellman
2004	DC United	Sporting KC	Columbus Crew	Brian Ching Eddie Johnson

TOP GOALSCORERS

CHRIS WONDOLOWSKI ★ 152 GOALS

FAB FACT!
In 2018, he became the first MLS player to score double figures for goals in nine consecutive seasons!

Chris Wondolowski

Three-time MLS top goalscorer and San Jose Earthquakes legend **CHRIS WONDOLOWSKI** really knows his way to the back of the net! As well as being the league's all-time top scorer, he also holds the record for most away MLS goals – and was voted the league's Most Valuable Player - or MVP - in 2012! Talking about MVPs, the award was renamed after MLS' second all-time top goalscorer **LANDON DONOVAN** in 2015. No player got more assists than the former LA Galaxy hero!

Landon Donovan

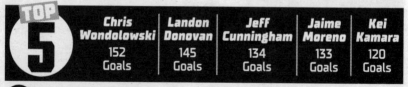

TOP 5	Chris Wondolowski	Landon Donovan	Jeff Cunningham	Jaime Moreno	Kei Kamara
	152 Goals	145 Goals	134 Goals	133 Goals	120 Goals

MOST APPEARANCES

NICK RIMANDO ★ 496 GAMES

FAB FACT!
Rimando lifted the MLS Cup with both DC United and Real Salt Lake!

Nick Rimando

He started his career with Miami Fusion, before deciding to sign for DC United, but **NICK RIMANDO** really wrote himself into the MLS history books after moving to Real Salt Lake in 2007! He's pulled off more saves and kept more clean sheets than any other goalkeeper, and been named in the MLS All-Star team five times. The outfielder with most MLS matches is another Real Salt Lake ledge - **KYLE BECKERMAN**. He also started at Miami Fusion and joined RSL in 2007, too!

Kyle Beckerman

TOP 5	Nick Rimando	Kyle Beckerman	Kevin Hartman	Chad Marshall	Jeff Larentowicz
	496 Games	473 Games	416 Games	409 Games	405 Games

CRAZY FACTS!

13

Ex-Toronto trickster Sebastian Giovinco holds the record for most goals scored from free-kicks!

2

Two teams are expected to join the league in 2020 – David Beckham's Inter Miami and Nashville SC!

31

Josef Martinez's 31 goals in 2018 for Atlanta set a new single-season record!

Zlatan Ibrahimovic scored a 40-yard half volley on his MLS debut for LA Galaxy!

26

Colombia CM Carlos Valderrama bagged a massive 26 assists in the 2000 season – an MLS record. Sick!

3 Wayne Rooney was named DC's captain just three matches after joining them!

STRANGE but true!

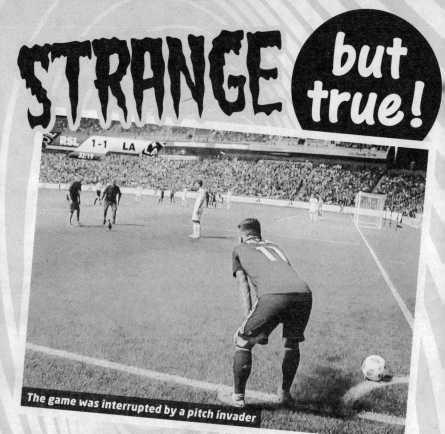

The game was interrupted by a pitch invader

Some of the world's best defenders and goalkeepers must have asked themselves what it takes to stop Zlatan Ibrahimovic from scoring... the simple answer? **A duck**! In **LA Galaxy**'s game with **Real Salt Lake** in September 2018, the animal flew onto the middle of the pitch and decided it was a good spot for a walk. Amazingly, the two sides didn't stop initially, and kept on playing for a couple of minutes with the duck just waddling around the pitch! Eventually, the game had to be paused – much to Ibra's annoyance – and FOUR stewards had to come onto the field to try and usher the beaked pitch invader away from trouble! The match ended up being a real 'quacker', with four goals scored in total!

The culprit

REST OF THE WORLD

There are some huge teams and epic ballers playing in other leagues around the world!

COPA LIBERTADORES

INDEPENDIENTE ★ 7 TITLES

The Copa Libertadores is like the South American version of the Champions League - it's open to the league winners of CONMEBOL member associations, plus teams finishing near the top of their respective leagues. Clubs from Argentina have more titles than any country, and Independiente, where Sergio Aguero began his wicked career, are the most successful side in the competition!

FAB FACT!

Independiente won the tournament four years in a row from 1972 to 1975!

DID YOU KNOW?

Copa Libertadores finals used to be played over two legs, with the 2019 final changing to a single game for the first time!

CHAMPIONS - LAST 15 SEASONS

YEAR	CHAMPIONS	RUNNERS-UP	FIRST LEG	SECOND LEG
2018	**River Plate**	Boca Juniors	2-2	3-1
2017	**Gremio**	Lanus	1-0	2-1
2016	**Atletico Nacional**	Independiente del Valle	1-1	1-0
2015	**River Plate**	UANL	0-0	3-0
2014	**San Lorenzo**	Nacional	1-1	1-0
2013	**Atletico Mineiro** Atl. won on pens	Olimpia	0-2	2-0
2012	**Corinthians**	Boca Juniors	1-1	2-0
2011	**Santos**	Penarol	0-0	2-1
2010	**Internacional**	Guadalajara	2-1	3-2
2009	**Estudiantes**	Cruzeiro	0-0	2-1
2008	**LDU Quito** Quito won on pens	Fluminense	4-2	1-3
2007	**Boca Juniors**	Gremio	3-0	2-0
2006	**Internacional**	Sao Paulo	2-1	2-2
2005	**Sao Paulo**	Atletico Paranaense	1-1	4-0
2004	**Once Caldas** Caldas won on pens	Boca Juniors	0-0	1-1

AUSTRALIA

MELBOURNE VICTORY & SYDNEY FC ★ 7 TITLES

FAB FACT!

Sydney and Melbourne's rivalry is known as The Big Blue – the colour of both team's kits!

CHAMPIONS 2017

HYUNDAI A-LEAGUE
CHAMPIONS
2017

HYUNDAI A-LEAGUE

Sydney FC

Just like in the MLS, the Australia A-League, which also features New Zealand's Wellington Phoenix, has two trophies on offer - one for the regular season league winners, and then a final series play-off between the top six! After the first 14 campaigns of the A-League's existence, **MELBOURNE VICTORY** and **SYDNEY FC** both had three regular season 'Premierships' as well as four final series 'Championships' to their name - a total combined of seven titles each. Wicked!

Melbourne Victory

TOP 5	Sydney FC	Melbourne Victory	Brisbane Roar	Central Coast Mariners	Adelaide United
	7 Titles	7 Titles	5 Titles	3 Titles	3 Titles

FAB FACT!
Guangzhou won seven titles in a row between 2011 and 2017!

Guangzhou Evergrande

🌐 The Chinese Super League was founded in 2004, and it's really grabbed headlines in the last decade with some big-name signings arriving to the league! **GUANGZHOU EVERGRANDE** had ex-Barcelona midfielder Paulinho in their squad for their 2017 campaign – the season they finished top of the table by six points and won title number seven! **SHANDONG LUNENG TAISHAN**, who snapped up Marouane Fellaini from Man. United, have the second most titles!

Marouane Fellaini

TOP 5	Guangzhou Evergrande	Shandong Luneng	Shanghai SIPG	Dalian Shide	Shenzhen Jianlibao
	7 Titles	3 Titles	1 Title	1 Title	1 Title

CRAZY FACTS!

50

Guangzhou Evergrande's academy is massive – it has 50 full-size pitches!

740+

Mexico's Liga MX record appearance maker is veteran keeper Oscar Perez – he's played over 700 games. Wowzers!

1o2

Neymar featured over 100 times for Santos in Brazil's Serie A between 2009 and 2013. Class!

50

SIPG Shanghai paid over £50 million for Chelsea's Oscar in December 2016!

5

Diego Maradona won five Argentina Primera Division top scorer prizes!

7

Marc Janko scored in seven consecutive A-League games in 2015!

STRANGE but true!

Alberto Gilardino

Loads of footy stars have tattoos these days – some weirder than others! Ex-Italy striker **Alberto Gilardino**'s one of Peppa Pig is up there, but Argentina goalkeeper **Gaspar Servio** is certainly another contender. . . Retired footy legend Diego Maradona took over as boss of his team Dorados de Sinaloa, who play in Mexico, in 2018 - and chose to make Servio his captain. In order to thank his gaffer, and show his somewhat freaky admiration, the keeper decided to get a tattoo of Maradona's face on his leg! It was certainly one way to make sure he stayed in Maradona's good books!

Gaspar Servio

WOMEN'S FOOTBALL

This section takes a look at both international and domestic women's football records!

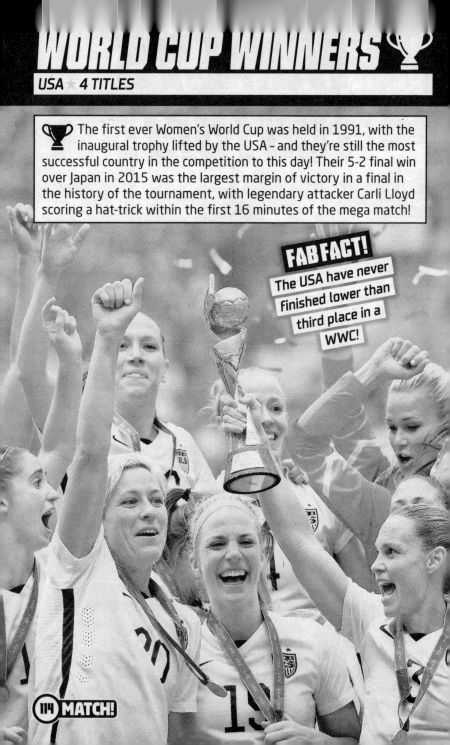

WORLD CUP WINNERS

USA ★ 4 TITLES

The first ever Women's World Cup was held in 1991, with the inaugural trophy lifted by the USA – and they're still the most successful country in the competition to this day! Their 5-2 final win over Japan in 2015 was the largest margin of victory in a final in the history of the tournament, with legendary attacker Carli Lloyd scoring a hat-trick within the first 16 minutes of the mega match!

FAB FACT!

The USA have never finished lower than third place in a WWC!

DID YOU KNOW?

In its very early days, the European Women's Championship was held every two years instead of every four like nowadays!

CHAMPIONS - LAST 15 TOURNAMENTS

YEAR	COMPETITION	HOSTS	CHAMPIONS	RUNNERS-UP
2019	World Cup	France	USA	Holland
2017	Euros	Holland	Holland	Denmark
2015	World Cup	Canada	USA	Japan
2013	Euros	Sweden	Germany	Norway
2011	World Cup	Germany	Japan	USA
2009	Euros	Finland	Germany	England
2007	World Cup	China	Germany	Brazil
2005	Euros	England	Germany	Norway
2003	World Cup	USA	Germany	Sweden
2001	Euros	Germany	Germany	Sweden
1999	World Cup	USA	USA	China
1997	Euros	Norway & Sweden	Germany	Italy
1995	World Cup	Sweden	Norway	Germany
1995	Euros	Germany	Germany	Sweden
1993	Euros	Italy	Norway	Italy

CHAMPIONS LEAGUE

LYON ★ 6 TITLES

Lyon

FAB FACT!
Lyon's Ada Hegerberg has busted over 40 Champions League nets. Ledge!

French giants **LYON** have lifted the most Women's Champions League trophies since the very first tournament in 2001-02! They've really dominated in recent seasons, too – they won the 2016, 2017, 2018 and 2019 titles, with the last two season's finals ending 4-1! German club **FRANKFURT** are currently second on the titles list, with their most recent victory coming in 2015 – they beat PSG 2-1 in the final, scoring a dramatic winner in the second minute of stoppage time!

Frankfurt

TOP 5	Lyon	Frankfurt	Umea	Turbine Potsdam	Wolfsburg
	6 Titles	4 Titles	2 Titles	2 Titles	2 Titles

WOMEN'S SUPER LEAGUE 🏆

ARSENAL ★ 3 TITLES

CHAMPIONS

BOREHAM OOD FOO

FAB FACT!
Arsenal won 54 points in 2018-19 – seven more than second-placed Man. City!

Arsenal celebrate winning the league

🏆 The FA Women's Super League is the highest league of women's football in England, which first started in 2010. Four teams have won the league title, but none more so than **ARSENAL**! They lifted their third league trophy in 2018-19, and sit one ahead of Chelsea and Liverpool. The Gunners also sit top of the charts in terms of Women's FA Cup victories, too – they've appeared in 16 finals since the tournament was founded back in 1970, more than any other team!

Arsenal lift the FA Cup

TOP 5

Arsenal	Southampton	Doncaster Belles	Everton	Chelsea
14 FA Cups	8 FA Cups	6 FA Cups	2 FA Cups	2 FA Cups

CRAZY FACTS!

13
USA's 13-0 win over Thailand in the 2019 WWC group stage was the biggest ever win at a Women's World Cup. Bonkers!

10
There were ten goals in the 1978 FA Cup final between Southampton and QPR – it ended 8-2 to The Saints!

30
Arsenal stars Beth Mead, Katie McCabe and Vivianne Miedema got 30 assists between them in 2018-19!

41
Brazil midfielder Formiga became the oldest player to feature at a WWC when she appeared at 41 in 2019!

11

Germany thrashed Argentina 11-0 in their 2007 WWC group stage game!

17

Marta's two goals at the 2019 WWC for Brazil took her tally to 17 in total – an all-time World Cup record. Sick!

STRANGE

but true!

Christine Sinclair takes a free-kick

Nobody wants to miss out on the opening game of a World Cup, just ask Canada's **Christine Sinclair**! Her country were playing Germany in their first match at the 2011 World Cup, and were losing 2-0 at half time. Not long after the break, she took an elbow to the face, and ended up with a broken nose! Medical staff told her to come off because it was dangerous to play on, but she managed to convince her gaffer to let her continue – and she went on to score one of the best free-kicks in Women's World Cup history. 'You need to have a broken leg to keep me out of World Cup games', she later said to FIFA!

Christine Sinclair

HALF-TIME QUIZ

See how much you've learnt from reading the first part of our wicked Records book!

TRUE or FALSE?

Are these real or made up? Put a tick or cross in the box!

1 Man. United were the first team to get their hands on the Premier League trophy in 1993!

2 The best ever EFL Championship points tally recorded by Reading was under 100!

3 Wigan lifted the awesome FA Cup trophy in 2010 after beating Man. City in the final!

4 No player's lifted more EFL Cup trophies than Argentina and Man. City star Sergio Aguero!

5 Alfredo Morelos won the Scottish Premiership top scorer prize in the 2018-19 campaign!

6 No superstar has busted more La Liga nets from penalties than Barcelona's Leo Messi!

WHO AM I?

Use the clues to work out the mystery star!

→ I played more than 600 league matches for my Serie A side!

→ I could play either from left-back or in central defence!

→ I won a massive 26 trophies for my club – what a hero!

WORDFIT

Fit the lethal goal machines into this awesome grid!

- Aduriz
- Benzema ✓
- Boyce
- Boyd
- Cunningham
- Donovan
- Drogba
- Hegerberg
- Henry
- Lacazette

- Lampard
- Murphy
- Rhodes
- Ronaldo
- Rooney
- Rush
- Sanchez
- Sharp
- Totti
- Zarra

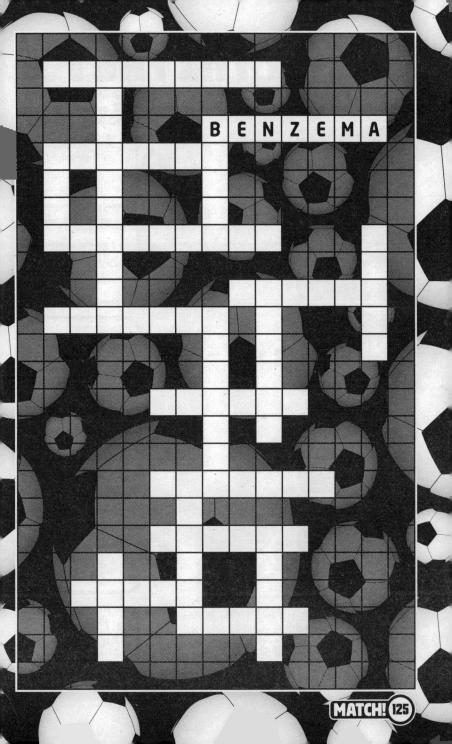

BENZEMA

MATCH THE FACTS!

Draw a line between the player and their corresponding fact!

Player		Fact
LIONEL MESSI 1	**A**	I've played in more EFL games than anyone!
LEE CAMP 2	**B**	I once broke my nose in a World Cup game!
RADAMEL FALCAO 3	**C**	I'm the most expensive player in the world!
CRISTIANO RONALDO 4	**D**	No-one's scored more CL goals than me!
NEYMAR 5	**E**	I'm the Europa League's all-time top scorer!
CHRISTINE SINCLAIR 6	**F**	I'm top of La Liga's all-time scorer charts!

WORLD CUP

It only happens every four years, but the FIFA World Cup is still the planet's most famous footy tournament!

It took them 28 years to get their hands on their first World Cup trophy, but Brazil are still the most successful country on the planet! They're the only nation to have played in every World Cup, hold the record for the most matches played and most victories, and are the only nation to have won the tournament on four different continents - once in Europe, once in South America, twice in North America and once in Asia. Class!

FAB FACT!

Brazil are one of just two nations to have won the trophy in back-to-back tournos – the other is Italy!

DID YOU KNOW?

Every time a nation wins the World Cup, they're allowed to add a star above their crest – that's why Brazil have five on theirs!

CHAMPIONS - LAST 15 TOURNAMENTS

YEAR	HOSTS	CHAMPIONS	RUNNER-UP	TOP SCORER
2018	Russia	France	Croatia	Harry Kane
2014	Brazil	Germany	Argentina	James Rodriguez
2010	South Africa	Spain	Holland	Thomas Muller David Villa Diego Forlan Wesley Sneijder
2006	Germany	Italy	France	Miroslav Klose
2002	South Korea & Japan	Brazil	Germany	Ronaldo
1998	France	France	Brazil	Davor Suker
1994	USA	Brazil	Italy	Hristo Stoichkov Oleg Salenko
1990	Italy	West Germany	Argentina	Salvatore Schillaci
1986	Mexico	Argentina	West Germany	Gary Lineker
1982	Spain	Italy	West Germany	Paolo Rossi
1978	Argentina	Argentina	Holland	Mario Kempes
1974	West Germany	West Germany	Holland	Grzegorz Lato
1970	Mexico	Brail	Italy	Gerd Muller
1966	England	England	West Germany	Eusebio
1962	Chile	Brazil	Czechoslovakia	Six players tied on four goals

MIROSLAV KLOSE ★ 16 GOALS

FAB FACT!

In 2006, Klose won the World Cup Golden Boot on home soil with five net-busters!

Miroslav Klose

⚽ Five goals on his debut World Cup in 2002 weren't enough to seal **MIROSLAV KLOSE** his first Golden Boot, but it set him up nicely to eventually become the tournament's all-time top scorer! After being a runner-up with Germany in 2002, then coming third in 2006 and 2010, the 2014 tourno was the pinnacle of his career – he won a gold World Cup medal and overtook **RONALDO** in the scoring charts. The Brazil star won the WC himself twice!

Ronaldo

TOP 5	Miroslav Klose	Ronaldo	Gerd Muller	Just Fontaine	Pele
	16 Goals	15 Goals	14 Goals	13 Goals	12 Goals

MOST APPEARANCES

FAB FACT!

Matthaus' five WC appearances is a joint record with Mexico's Rafael Marquez and Antonio Carbajal!

Lothar Matthaus

Widely regarded as one of the greatest midfielders ever to grace the game, **LOTHAR MATTHAUS** was captain of West Germany when they lifted the World Cup in 1990! That was the third WC competition he'd featured in, but he went on to play at the 1994 and 1998 tournaments too, featuring in more WC games than any other player! Fellow countryman **MIROSLAV KLOSE** appeared in one less cup, but almost reached the same number of games!

Miroslav Klose

TOP 5	Lothar Matthaus	Miroslav Klose	Paolo Maldini	Diego Maradona	Uwe Seeler
	25 Games	24 Games	23 Games	21 Games	21 Games

CRAZY FACTS!

2

In 2018, Kylian Mbappe became just the second teenager to score in a WC final - alongside Pele!

3

No team has lost more World Cup penalty shootouts than England!

 132 MATCH!

2

Luis Monti played in two World Cup final matches with two different nations – Argentina and Italy!

6

The defending champs have been dumped out in the first round six times. Poor form!

13

France's Just Fontaine scored all 13 of his World Cup goals in a single tournament!

3

Holland have reached the final the most times without ever lifting the epic trophy!

STRANGE but true!

Josip Simunic makes a tackle

Everyone knows about Diego Maradona's mad 'Hand of God' goal v The Three Lions in 1986, but we're going to explore another crazy World Cup moment involving England – but this time a referee! **Graham Poll** was in charge of Croatia's match against Australia at World Cup 2006 and, after booking Croatia defender **Josip Simunic** for a foul in the 61st minute, he then booked him again in the 90th – but forgot to send him off! It was only after he'd blown the final whistle, and Simunic decided to push him, that Poll handed the player his third yellow – and this time a red! Thankfully, the decision didn't have time to impact the match!

Graham Poll

EUROPEAN CHAMPIONSHIP

Every four years, a new European champion is crowned the best nation on the continent!

GERMANY & SPAIN ★ 3 TITLES

Ten different countries have won the European Championship, but none more so than giants Germany and Spain! The two mega nations have won the tourno three times each, but France are on their trails with two trophies. Les Bleus came really close to matching their rivals in the most recent Euros in 2016, but they were beaten on home soil by Portugal in the final after extra time. Gutting!

FAB FACT!

The Euros are the second most watched football tourno on the planet after the World Cup!

DID YOU KNOW?

For the first time ever, Euro 2020 will be held all across Europe, in 12 different cities and countries! It's to mark the comp's 60th anniversary!

CHAMPIONS - LAST 15 TOURNAMENTS

YEAR	HOSTS	CHAMPIONS	RUNNER-UP	TOP SCORER
2016	France	Portugal	France	Antoine Griezmann
2012	Poland & Ukraine	Spain	Italy	Six players tied on three goals
2008	Austria & Switzerland	Spain	Germany	David Villa
2004	Portugal	Greece	Portugal	Milan Baros
2000	Belgium & Holland	France	Italy	Patrick Kluivert Savo Milosevic
1996	England	Germany	Czech Republic	Alan Shearer
1992	Sweden	Denmark	Germany	Four players tied on three goals
1988	West Germany	Holland	Soviet Union	Marco van Basten
1984	France	France	Spain	Michel Platini
1980	Italy	West Germany	Belgium	Klaus Allofs
1976	Yugoslavia	Czechoslovakia	West Germany	Dieter Muller
1972	Belgium	West Germany	Soviet Union	Gerd Muller
1968	Italy	Italy	Yugoslavia	Dragan Dzajic
1964	Spain	Spain	Soviet Union	Jesus Pereda Ferenc Bene Dezso Novak
1960	France	Soviet Union	Yugoslavia	Five players tied on two goals

FAB FACT!
Platini scored the first goal in the 1984 final v Spain – they went on to win 2-0!

Michel Platini

Nicknamed 'The King' in his home country, **MICHEL PLATINI** was an awesome attacking midfielder for France! Incredibly, he only ever appeared in one European Championship, but he tore it up as captain! He scored nine goals, three times as many as any other player, as Les Bleus went on to lift the 1984 trophy on home soil! **CRISTIANO RONALDO** caught up with him at Euro 2016, though - the legendary forward bagged three goals in France to help take his team to the title!

Cristiano Ronaldo

TOP 5	Michel Platini	Cristiano Ronaldo	Alan Shearer	Antoine Griezmann	Wayne Rooney
	9 Goals	9 Goals	7 Goals	6 Goals	6 Goals

MOST APPEARANCES

CRISTIANO RONALDO ★ 21 GAMES

FAB FACT!
At Euro 2016, Cristiano became the first player to score at four different Euro Championships!

Cristiano Ronaldo

The 2004 European Championship, held in Portugal, was where legend **CRISTIANO RONALDO** was to score his first ever international goal! It came in a group stage loss to eventual champions Greece – the same country that narrowly beat the hosts in the final! C-Ron was named in the Team Of The Tournament in 2004, and again in 2012 and 2016! Germany's **BASTIAN SCHWEINSTEIGER**, who was runner up in 2008, is currently second on the list for Euro appearances!

Bastian Schweinsteiger

TOP 5	Cristiano Ronaldo	Bastian Schweinsteiger	Gianluigi Buffon	Andres Iniesta	Cesc Fabregas
	21 Games	18 Games	17 Games	16 Games	16 Games

CRAZY FACTS!

13

Germany thrashed San Marino 13-0 in a qualifying game back in 2006!

23

No player's scored more goals in Euro qualifying than Republic Of Ireland legend Robbie Keane!

7

Portugal have participated in seven different Euros, and have made it past the first round every single time. Sick!

108

There were 108 nets busted at Euro 2016 - more than at any other previous tournament!

24

France´s Eric Abidal holds the record for fastest sending off - he was dismissed after 24 minutes in their game v Italy in 2008!

1

At Euro 2016, Taulant and Granit Xhaka became the first siblings to play against each other in Euro history - Taulant played for Albania and Granit turned out for Switzerland!

STRANGE but true!

Cristiano Ronaldo

Portugal captain **Cristiano Ronaldo** was understandably the hero as the country lifted their first ever major international trophy at Euro 2016, but one of the most memorable moments of the final was actually when he got injured! The then-Real Madrid forward started to cry as he realised he wouldn't be able to continue playing and, to make matters worse, a **giant moth** decided to land in his eye! Groundsmen had left the floodlights on overnight and thousands of the insect plagued the stadium prior to kick-off. They could be seen annoying players during the game, but the one that landed on CR7 was clearly desperate for fame!

The pesky moth

ENGLAND

The Three Lions are one of the two oldest national teams in football – alongside Scotland!

COMPETITIVE RECORD

WORLD CUPS AND EUROPEAN CHAMPIONSHIPS

🏆 England first appeared at a World Cup back in 1950, and have qualified for 15 in total - tied in sixth for number of WC appearances! While their run in 2018 was well exciting, their best ever display was in 1966, when they lifted the trophy on home soil after beating West Germany 4-2 in the final! In terms of the Euros, The Three Lions' best ever finish is third - it's happened two times, in 1968 and at home in 1996!

FAB FACT!

Only three countries have appeared in more European Championships than England!

FIFA WORLD RANKING – LAST TEN YEARS

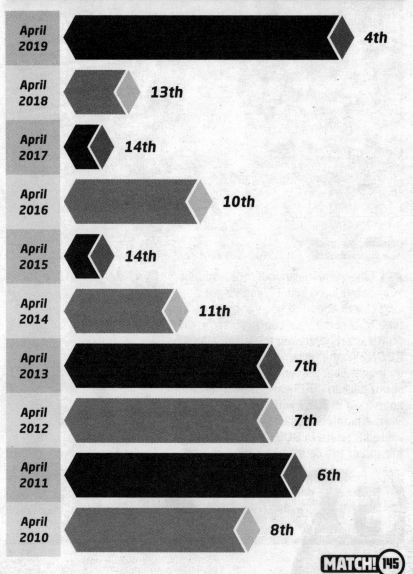

April 2019	4th
April 2018	13th
April 2017	14th
April 2016	10th
April 2015	14th
April 2014	11th
April 2013	7th
April 2012	7th
April 2011	6th
April 2010	8th

TOP GOALSCORERS

WAYNE ROONEY ★ 53 GOALS

FAB FACT!
Wazza became England's youngest scorer when he netted against Macedonia in 2003!

Wayne Rooney

When you make your international debut aged just 17, you've got a long career ahead of you – and plenty of time to become your country's top scorer! That's what happened to striker **WAYNE ROONEY**, who became The Three Lions' youngest ever player when he made his debut back in 2003 – and the nation's top goalscorer in 2015 with a penalty against Switzerland! He replaced another ex-Man United forward in **BOBBY CHARLTON** at the top of the country's scoring charts!

Bobby Charlton

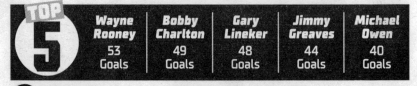

TOP 5	Wayne Rooney	Bobby Charlton	Gary Lineker	Jimmy Greaves	Michael Owen
	53 Goals	49 Goals	48 Goals	44 Goals	40 Goals

MOST APPEARANCES

PETER SHILTON ★ 125 GAMES

Peter Shilton

FAB FACT!

Shilton also holds the all-time record for most competitive games in world football!

If you're looking for an impressive cap collection, **PETER SHILTON** is your man! The legendary goalkeeper, who played for 11 different teams during his incredible career, holds another wicked record, too – no other goalie has kept more clean sheets in World Cup tournos than him! **WAYNE ROONEY** came close to breaking Shilton's appearance record for England, but put an end to his Three Lions career in 2018 after his final match v the USA – they won that contest 3-0!

Wayne Rooney

TOP 5

Peter Shilton	Wayne Rooney	David Beckham	Steven Gerrard	Bobby Moore
125 Games	120 Games	115 Games	114 Games	108 Games

CRAZY FACTS!

No player has made more appearances off the bench for England than super-sub striker Jermain Defoe!

35

2000

The last English goalscorer at the old Wembley stadium was actually a centre-back - former Arsenal defender Tony Adams!

2

No player has had a shorter England career than Martin Kelly – he played just over two minutes v Norway in 2012, and never won another cap!

19

Theo Walcott became the youngest player to score a hat-trick, when he did it v Croatia in 2008 aged 19!

7

When England thrashed San Marino 8-0 in March 2013, there were seven different goalscorers!

8

Gareth Barry is a popular guy – he played under eight different bosses, including caretaker managers, during his epic Three Lions career!

STRANGE but true!

Pickles

The 1966 World Cup in England was obviously a massive event for the country, but it didn't start particularly smoothly! The famous **Jules Rimet trophy** was being held at an exhibition in London before the tourno got underway, with guards making sure it was kept safe. But, one day, they realised someone had broken in and stolen it! The news spread all across the world, with the police desperately searching for it, but it wasn't them that eventually found it – it was a man walking his dog called **Pickles**! After saving the day, Pickles became a celeb – and even made it onto TV and starred in a film!

Jules Rimet trophy

SCOTLAND

Scotland's first ever international football match was against England way back in 1872!

FAB FACT!

Scotland are hosting four games at Euro 2020 – three in the groups and one Last 16 clash!

Scotland hold the unfortunate record of qualifying for the most World Cups without then getting past the first round! They've appeared in eight World Cup tournaments, including five consecutively between 1974 and 1990, and have missed out on getting past round one three times because of goal difference! They've had the same fate in European Championships, too - they've qualified for two Euros, but been knocked out in the first round in both competitions!

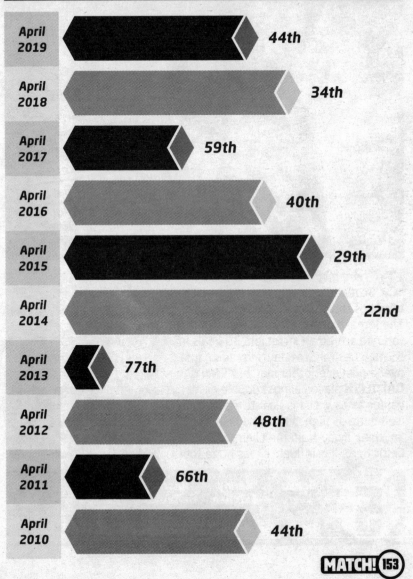

FIFA WORLD RANKING – LAST TEN YEARS

- April 2019 — 44th
- April 2018 — 34th
- April 2017 — 59th
- April 2016 — 40th
- April 2015 — 29th
- April 2014 — 22nd
- April 2013 — 77th
- April 2012 — 48th
- April 2011 — 66th
- April 2010 — 44th

TOP GOALSCORERS

FAB FACT!
Law's the only Scottish player to win the Ballon d'Or award – he got it in 1964!

Denis Law

There might be a tie at the top of Scotland's scoring charts, but **DENIS LAW** has the better goal-to-game ratio! The lethal ex-Man. City and Man. United forward scored an incredible 30 goals in 55 matches for Scotland, averaging just over a goal ever other match! **KENNY DALGLISH** played almost double as many games as Law, so his goal-to-game ratio isn't quite as high, but that doesn't take anything away from the Liverpool and Celtic hero – his influence was huge too!

Kenny Dalglish

TOP 5	Denis Law	Kenny Dalglish	Hughie Gallacher	Lawrie Reilly	Ally McCoist
	30 Goals	30 Goals	24 Goals	22 Goals	19 Goals

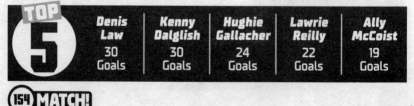

MOST APPEARANCES

KENNY DALGLISH ★ 102 GAMES

FAB FACT!
'King Kenny' was introduced to the Scottish Football Hall Of Fame in 2004!

Kenny Dalglish

KENNY DALGLISH is the only man in Scotland's history to have won over 100 caps for the country, so he's obviously got real legendary status! He scored some quality goals for the nation, including one at the 1978 World Cup in their 3-2 win over eventual runners-up Holland, and the winner against England at Hampden Park in 1976 with a nutmeg! Goalkeeper **JIM LEIGHTON** came close to reaching a century of caps, and appeared in four of Scotland's World Cup squads!

Jim Leighton

TOP 5	Kenny Dalglish	Jim Leighton	Darren Fletcher	Alex McLeish	Paul McStay
	102 Games	91 Games	80 Games	77 Games	76 Games

CRAZY FACTS! 2018

CM Scott McTominay was born in England, but made his Scotland debut in 2018 after receiving advice from Sir Alex Ferguson!

85

Scotland played 26 games in the 1880s – and they won a huge 85% of them!

6

Six years before being made Scotland captain, Andy Robertson was playing in Scotland's third tier. Sick progress!

Scotland reached 13th in the FIFA rankings in 2007 after beating WC runners-up France twice!

13

3

Denis Law scored two hat-tricks against Norway in the same year - 1963!

10

Brazil are the only country Scotland have faced in double figures but never beaten!

STRANGE but true!

Hampden Park

When you look up the capacity of **Scotland**'s national stadium **Hampden Park**, you'll see that it holds close to 52,000 for football matches... But did you know that it holds the record for the highest attended international match in Europe? In 1937, when England travelled north to face their rivals in a British Home Championship showdown, Hampden Park wasn't a seated stadium - fans stood at matches, so there was more room to pack people in! The official attendance for that match was counted as a whopping 149,415, which set a new world record at the time, but it's actually predicted that over 180,000 were at the stadium on the day - loads of fans managed to gain entry without a ticket. Nowadays, it's all-seated!

STADIUMS

This category checks out the biggest and best stadiums from all across the planet!

EUROPE

NOU CAMP ★ 99,354 CAPACITY

Flying the flag for Europe is Barcelona's Nou Camp – officially the biggest stadium on the continent! What's more, the Catalan club are currently preparing to renovate and expand the awesome ground, meaning that the intended new capacity for the 2023-24 season is actually 105,000! In second place is England's national stadium Wembley, which boasts having more toilets than any other venue in the world – 2,618. That doesn't mean there aren't queues!

FAB FACT!

The Nou Camp has a chapel inside the stadium, near the players' tunnel!

DID YOU KNOW?

Croke Park is now used for Gaelic games, but Republic Of Ireland have used it for home internationals in the past too!

BIGGEST STADIUMS IN EUROPE

STADIUM	CAPACITY	COUNTRY	TEAM	OPENED
Nou Camp	99,354	Spain	Barcelona	1957
Wembley	90,000	England	England National Team	2007
Croke Park	82,300	Rep. Of Ireland	Rep. Of Ireland National Team	1884
Signal Iduna Park	81,365	Germany	Borussia Dortmund	1974
Santiago Bernabeu	81,044	Spain	Real Madrid	1947
Luzhniki Stadium	81,004	Russia	Russia National Team	1956
Stade de France	80,698	France	France National Team	1998
San Siro	80,018	Italy	AC and Inter Milan	1926
Ataturk Olympic Stadium	76,761	Turkey	Turkey National Team	2002
Allianz Arena	75,000	Germany	Bayern Munich	2005
Old Trafford	74,994	England	Man. United	1910
Millennium Stadium	74,500	Wales	Wales National Team	1999
Olympiastadion	74,475	Germany	Hertha Berlin	1936
Stadio Olimpico	70,634	Italy	Roma and Lazio	1937
Olimpiyskiy Stadium	70,050	Ukraine	Ukraine National Team	1923

FAB FACT!

The Rose Bowl Stadium was the venue for the Women's World Cup final in 1999!

Rose Bowl Stadium

Found in California, the **ROSE BOWL STADIUM** is the only footy ground in North or South America with a current capacity of over 90,000! It was the home of MLS side LA Galaxy between 1996 and 2002, but nowadays is just used by the US Men's national team. It's hosted some pretty big games, too – the 1994 World Cup final, won by Brazil, was held there! The **ESTADIO AZTECA**, home of Mexico's national team, Club America and Cruz Azul is also absolutely enormous!

Estadio Azteca

TOP 5

Rose Bowl Stadium	Estadio Azteca	MetLife Stadium	Estadio Monumental	AT&T Stadium
90,888 Capacity	87,523 Capacity	82,500 Capacity	80,093 Capacity	80,000 Capacity

FNB Stadium

FAB FACT!
The record attendance at the FNB was a match between Kaizer Chiefs and Orlando Pirates in 2015 – 94,807!

The **FNB STADIUM**, also known as Soccer City by fans, is a jaw-dropping ground in Johannesburg, South Africa, used by the national team and famous club Kaizer Chiefs! As well as hosting the 2010 World Cup opener in the country, it was also the venue for the final between Holland and Spain – and its cool design is supposed to represent an African pot! It's the biggest stadium in Africa, followed by the **BORG EL ARAB STADIUM**, which hosts the Egypt national football team!

Borg El Arab Stadium

TOP 5	FNB Stadium	Borg El Arab Stadium	Stade des Martyrs	Cairo Stadium	Stade Mohammed V
	94,736 Capacity	86,000 Capacity	80,000 Capacity	75,000 Capacity	67,000 Capacity

CRAZY FACTS!

2000

The Ottmar Hitzfeld Stadium, located in the Swiss Alps, is 2,000 metres above sea level – and is reached via a trip on a cable car!

2,760

Bayern's Allianz Arena has 2,760 panels, which can light up at night!

1884

Between 1884 and 1892, Anfield was actually the home of Everton - Liverpool's massive rivals. Wow!

2007

Beijing's National Stadium, which was built in 2007, is designed like a bird's nest. Cool!

360

Atlanta United's awesome Mercedes-Benz Stadium has a 360-degree HD video screen in the centre of the stadium for fans to watch!

3,601

Bolivia's national team play at the Estadio Hernando Siles - one of the highest grounds in the world at 3,601 metres above sea level!

STRANGE but true!

Estadio Municipal de Braga

There are some really bizarre stadiums in the world, like **The Float at Marina Bay Stadium** in Singapore that floats on an island, or **Vozdovac Belgrade**'s ground that was built on top of a shopping centre! Perhaps the weirdest one currently used by a big European club is Braga's **Estadio Municipal de Braga**, in Portugal! The Primeira Division side's stadium, which was built in 2003 for the 2004 Euros and holds 30,000 fans, was carved into the side of a mountain – with the scoreboard mounted on a cliff at the edge of the ground! We're not sure how many balls burst a year by crashing into the rocks…

Marina Bay

Vozdovac Belgrade's ground

WALES

GORAU · CHWARAE · CYD · CHWARAE

The Dragons are the third oldest international team in the world, playing their first game in 1876!

COMPETITIVE RECORD 🏆

WORLD CUPS AND EUROPEAN CHAMPIONSHIPS

🏆 Wales have qualified for two major international tournaments – one World Cup and one European Championship! Their only ever WC appearance came back in 1958 – they came second in their group but were eliminated by eventual winners Brazil in the quarter-finals. They went one better at Euro 2016, though! After topping a group with England, they then beat Northern Ireland and Belgium, before being knocked out by the champions Portugal in the semis!

FAB FACT!

The Dragons progressed further than any other British team at Euro 2016!

FIFA WORLD RANKING – LAST TEN YEARS

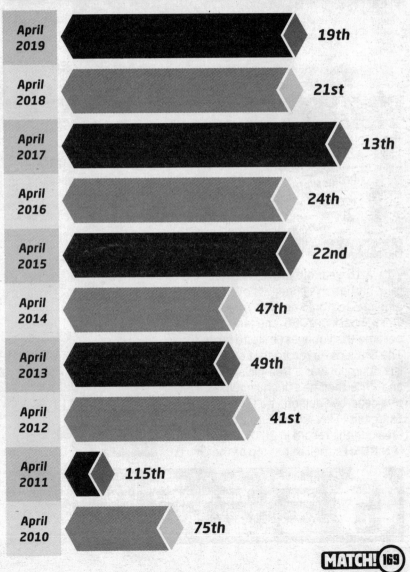

April 2019	19th
April 2018	21st
April 2017	13th
April 2016	24th
April 2015	22nd
April 2014	47th
April 2013	49th
April 2012	41st
April 2011	115th
April 2010	75th

TOP GOALSCORERS

GARETH BALE ★ 31 GOALS

FAB FACT!
The powerful winger broke Wales' goal record with a hat-trick against China in 2018!

Gareth Bale

⚽ A 16-year-old **GARETH BALE** was his nation's youngest ever player when he featured against Trinidad & Tobago back in 2006, and later that year became the youngest hero to score for The Dragons – a record that still stands! His first goal was a free-kick v Slovakia, and since then he's been known as a bit of a dead-ball demon – he scored another FK against Slovakia at Euro 2016 too! By breaking the record in 2018, Bale ended **IAN RUSH**'s spell at the top of the charts!

Ian Rush

TOP 5	Gareth Bale	Ian Rush	Trevor Ford	Ivor Allchurch	Dean Saunders
	31 Goals	28 Goals	23 Goals	23 Goals	22 Goals

MOST APPEARANCES

CHRIS GUNTER ★ 95 GAMES

FAB FACT!
The ex-Tottenham defender played over 20 times for The Dragons' youth teams, too!

Chris Gunter

Being able to play both left-back and right-back makes you a dream for an international manager wanting versatility in his squad – and it's certainly worked well for **CHRIS GUNTER**! The attacking full-back was a key member of the squad that got to the semis of Euro 2016, and he was even named Welsh Footballer Of The Year in 2017! Gunter overtook legendary former Everton GK **NEVILLE SOUTHALL**, who was briefly Wales' caretaker boss in 1999, in 2018!

Neville Southall

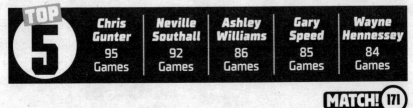

TOP 5	Chris Gunter	Neville Southall	Ashley Williams	Gary Speed	Wayne Hennessey
	95 Games	92 Games	86 Games	85 Games	84 Games

CRAZY FACTS!

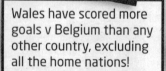

20

Wales have scored more goals v Belgium than any other country, excluding all the home nations!

1881

The Dragons' first ever international victory came against rivals England!

Manager Ryan Giggs won over 60 caps for the country during his playing career!

64

15

They played in 15 games in the 1940s, but they didn't draw any of them. Weird!

16

In 2013, awesome attacker Harry Wilson snatched Gareth Bale's record as Wales' youngest player!

9

Wales' worst ever loss came against Scotland - they lost 9-0 back in 1878!

STRANGE but true!

Option 1

Team photos don't have to be dull, you know! Back in 2016, people started noticing that **Wales** weren't sticking to the typical six-at-the-back and five-at-the-front line-up for their team snaps – for one game against Georgia they had eight players kneeling down in the front row! In other games, they'd go for a lop-sided look – so more players would be on the right-hand side of the picture than the left! It turns out that, at the beginning, they just weren't very good at team photos, but once they realised, they decided to make a joke out of it and started doing weird formations. Even today, it's a bit of a tradition for The Dragons!

Option 2

REPUBLIC OF IRELAND

The Republic Of Ireland have two cool nicknames – The Boys in Green and The Green Army!

COMPETITIVE RECORD

WORLD CUPS AND EUROPEAN CHAMPIONSHIPS

The Green Army have qualified for three World Cups in their history, but they can claim a 100% success rate of getting out of their groups! They reached the Last 16 in both 1994 and 2002, but their best WC campaign was defo in 1990 in Italy - they made it to the quarter-finals! They've also qualified for three Euro Championships, but they've only got out of their group once – in 2016. They were a goal ahead after two minutes against France in the Last 16, but eventually suffered a 2-1 defeat to the hosts!

FAB FACT!

ROI's Aviva Stadium will host four fixtures at Euro 2020, including one Last 16 clash!

DID YOU KNOW?

The manager with most games in charge of Republic Of Ireland is actually a former England international – Jack Charlton!

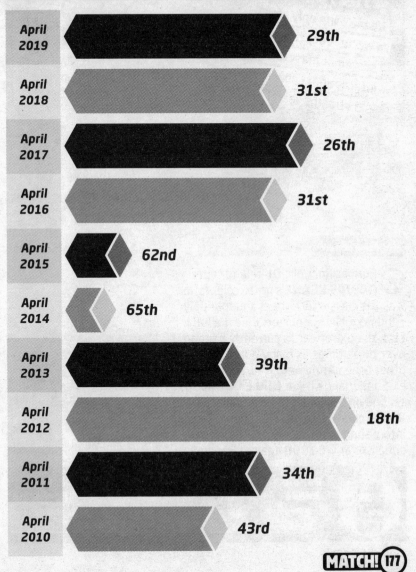

FIFA WORLD RANKING – LAST TEN YEARS

April 2019	29th
April 2018	31st
April 2017	26th
April 2016	31st
April 2015	62nd
April 2014	65th
April 2013	39th
April 2012	18th
April 2011	34th
April 2010	43rd

ROBBIE KEANE ★ 68 GOALS

FAB FACT!

Keane's the only star in world footy to have scored at least one international goal in 19 straight years!

Robbie Keane

🔵 Former Republic Of Ireland captain **ROBBIE KEANE**'s go-to celebration was the classic cartwheel and roly-poly – and Republic supporters saw it a lot! In fact, the ex-forward's currently bagged over three times as many goals as any other Green Army hero! Tall, six-foot four ex-Sunderland striker **NIALL QUINN** sits second on the list, and he actually played for the country at three of their six major international tournaments, scoring an equaliser at WC 1990 against Holland!

Niall Quinn

TOP 5	Robbie Keane	Niall Quinn	Frank Stapleton	John Aldridge	Tony Cascarino
	68 Goals	21 Goals	20 Goals	19 Goals	19 Goals

MOST APPEARANCES

ROBBIE KEANE ★ **146 GAMES**

FAB FACT!
Given's the longest-serving ROI player – there were 20 years between his debut and actual retirement!

Shay Given

It's that man again! **ROBBIE KEANE** doesn't just hold the ROI record for most goals, he's also the nation's most-capped player – and one of only six to have reached a ton! We're going to shout out to **SHAY GIVEN**, though – the former Man. City, Newcastle and Aston Villa GK is the second-most capped player, but the most-capped goalkeeper! Given made his debut before old team-mate Keane, but he retired in 2012, only to come out of retirement a year later. He missed it!

Robbie Keane

TOP 5	Robbie Keane	Shay Given	John O'Shea	Kevin Kilbane	Steve Staunton
	146 Games	134 Games	118 Games	110 Games	102 Games

CRAZY FACTS!

3 David Kelly is the only player to score a hat-trick on his debut for Republic!

2 Former midfielder Noel Campbell was once sent off two minutes after coming on against Bulgaria in 1977!

1 Shane Long was the first star to have played both hurling and international football at Croke Park!

5 Giovanni Trapattoni's one of five men not born in the Republic to have managed them!

Their biggest victory came against Malta - they thrashed them 8-0 back in 1983! **8**

ROI won the 2011 Nations Cup - a one-off tourno between them, Northern Ireland, Wales and Scotland. Wicked!

STRANGE but true!

Rice for ROI

Award ceremonies can take a long time to organise, and people are often asked to vote for their nominees way in advance of the actual event. That's how current England central midfielder **Declan Rice** won Republic Of Ireland's **Young Player Of The Year** prize – less than a month after confirming that he'd actually be switching to play for England! The reason he was allowed to change allegiance was because he'd only played in friendlies for the Republic, but the Football Association Of Ireland decided that they should honour the votes anyway – hence why Rice is a holder of The Boys In Green's best young player prize!

Rice for England

NORTHERN IRELAND

The Green and White Army's crest is actually made up of gold, blue and white!

COMPETITIVE RECORD

WORLD CUPS AND EUROPEAN CHAMPIONSHIPS

Northern Ireland have made it to four major international tournaments - World Cups 1958, 1982 and 1986, plus the 2016 European Championship! They made it out of their group in all but one of those competitions, but have never got further than the quarter-finals, or second round. In their most recent appearance - the 2016 Euros - they advanced to the knockouts as one of the best third-placed sides, but were eliminated by fellow home nation Wales 1-0. Gareth McAuley scored an own goal in the second half!

FAB FACT!

At the 1982 World Cup, Northern Ireland beat hosts Spain and even topped their group!

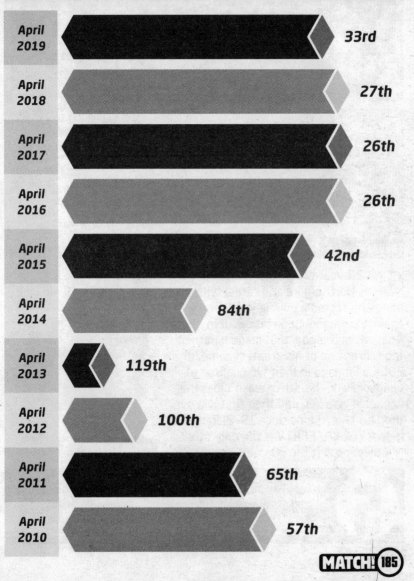

FIFA WORLD RANKING - LAST TEN YEARS

April 2019	33rd
April 2018	27th
April 2017	26th
April 2016	26th
April 2015	42nd
April 2014	84th
April 2013	119th
April 2012	100th
April 2011	65th
April 2010	57th

DAVID HEALY ★ 36 GOALS

FAB FACT!
Healy hit 13 goals in the 2008 European Championship qualifying campaign – a joint-high record!

David Healy

A 20-year-old **DAVID HEALY** began his Northern Ireland career with a bang – he scored a double in a friendly against Luxembourg on his debut in 2000! Apart from the goal that made him their top scorer, one of his greatest came in 2005 v England in their WC qualifier at Windsor Park – his strike wasn't just the winner, it also secured their first win over the The Three Lions since 1972! Rangers hero **KYLE LAFFERTY** is the only other NIR player to hit the 20 goals landmark!

Kyle Lafferty

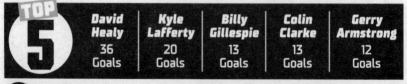

TOP 5	David Healy	Kyle Lafferty	Billy Gillespie	Colin Clarke	Gerry Armstrong
	36 Goals	20 Goals	13 Goals	13 Goals	12 Goals

MOST APPEARANCES

FAB FACT!
The incredible shot-stopper won the FA Cup with north London rivals Spurs and Arsenal!

Pat Jennings

Legendary keeper **PAT JENNINGS** is a member of a fairly exclusive group of players to have won trophies for both north London rivals Spurs and Arsenal! He might not have won anything for Nothern Ireland, but he'll forever be in their history books for winning 119 caps in a 22-year period. Another hero to have been involved in his country's footballing history for over two decades is defender **AARON HUGHES**. The centre-back is also the outfield player with most caps. Class!

Aaron Hughes

TOP 5	Pat Jennings	Aaron Hughes	Steven Davis	David Healy	Mal Donaghy
	119 Games	112 Games	111 Games	95 Games	91 Games

CRAZY FACTS!

3 David Healy scored three in a historic 3-2 win in 2006 against a Spain side with Sergio Ramos, Fernando Torres, Xavi, Cesc Fabregas and David Villa!

6 They've played France six times and never won - they've lost four of those games, too!

41 Pat Jennings retired from club footy in 1985, but continued playing for Northern Ireland until he was 41. Total legend!

31

Steven Davis played a whopping 31 times for Northern Ireland's youth teams. Patient!

17

Norman Whiteside broke Pele's record as the youngest ever player to appear at a WC, when he made his debut at 17 in 1982!

1964

Jennings made his international debut in the same game as another top legend - winger George Best!

STRANGE but true!

Will Grigg

Sean Kennedy

When Wigan fan **Sean Kennedy** made up a chant for Northern Ireland striker **Will Grigg** in May 2016, he never would've expected it to become so famous! The song, with the really catchy chorus 'Will Grigg's on fire, your defence is terrified', was an instant hit among both Wigan and Northern Ireland fans, and was perfectly timed ahead of the Euro 2016 Championship! It became mega famous, with The Green and White Army signing it loudly and proudly at all their matches in France, and electric band Blonde releasing it as an official song – it even made the UK's Official iTunes Top Ten! After seeing his song chanted by Nothern Ireland fans all summer, Kennedy was then given a free Wigan season ticket for 2016-17 for becoming such a success!

OTHER NATIONS

Check out some of the other teams and tournament records from around the planet!

The CONMEBOL Copa America, which was founded in 1916, is the oldest international footy competition on the planet! It determines the continental champs of South America, although teams from North America and Asia have also participated since the 1990s – Japan and Qatar were the invited teams in 2019! The most successful country is currently Uruguay, who won the first ever tournament, although Argentina are just behind them on 14!

FAB FACT!

Uruguay won six of the first ten Copa America trophies!

DID YOU KNOW?

The 2016 Copa America was a 100-year special featuring 16 teams, including the likes of USA, Haiti and Jamaica!

CHAMPIONS - LAST 15 TOURNAMENTS

YEAR	HOSTS	CHAMPIONS	RUNNERS-UP	TOP SCORER
2019	Brazil	Brazil	Peru	Paolo Guerrero Everton
2016	USA	Chile	Argentina	Eduardo Vargas
2015	Chile	Chile	Argentina	Eduardo Vargas Paolo Guerrero
2011	Argentina	Uruguay	Paraguay	Paolo Guerrero
2007	Venezuela	Brazil	Argentina	Robinho
2004	Peru	Brazil	Argentina	Adriano
2001	Colombia	Colombia	Mexico	Victor Aristizabal
1999	Paraguay	Brazil	Uruguay	Ronaldo Rivaldo
1997	Bolivia	Brazil	Bolivia	Luis Hernandez
1995	Uruguay	Uruguay	Brazil	Gabriel Batistuta Luis Garcia
1993	Ecuador	Argentina	Mexico	Jose Dolgetta
1991	Chile	Argentina	Brazil	Gabriel Batistuta
1989	Brazil	Brazil	Uruguay	Bebeto
1987	Argentina	Uruguay	Chile	Arnoldo Iguaran
1983	Various	Uruguay	Brazil	Carlos Aguilera Jorge Burruchaga Roberto Dinamite

GOLD CUP

MEXICO ★ 8 TITLES

FAB FACT!
Mexico are the only nation to have won the competition three times in a row!

Mexico

Formed in 1991 to replace the CONCACAF Championship, and held every two years, the Gold Cup is the main association football tourno for nations in North America, Central America and the Caribbean - though guests from other continents have appeared, too! **MEXICO** are the most successful nation, although USA are hot on their trail with six wins! Legendary Stars and Stripes attacker **LANDON DONOVAN** is the top scorer in Gold Cup history - he netted five in 2013!

Landon Donovan

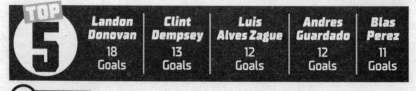

TOP 5	Landon Donovan	Clint Dempsey	Luis Alves Zague	Andres Guardado	Blas Perez
	18 Goals	13 Goals	12 Goals	12 Goals	11 Goals

AFRICA CUP OF NATIONS

EGYPT ★ 7 TITLES

FAB FACT!
Egypt won three competitions in a row in 2006, 2008 and 2010!

Egypt

Nowadays, 24 teams compete in the Africa Cup of Nations, but there were only three teams in the first ever tournament in 1957 – Egypt, Sudan and Ethiopia! **EGYPT** won that edition, and they've since lifted more trophies than any other nation, with 2017 champions Cameroon in second place with five. It's a Cameroon legend that sits at the top of the all-time scorer charts, though – former Barcelona goal machine **SAMUEL ETO'O**, who hit five in 2006 and 2008!

Samuel Eto'o

TOP 5	Samuel Eto'o	Laurent Pokou	Rashidi Yekini	Hassan El Shazly	Didier Drogba
	18 Goals	14 Goals	13 Goals	12 Goals	11 Goals

CRAZY FACTS!

5
Ex-Ivory Coast ace Laurent Pokou once scored five goals in one AFCON match against Ethiopia in 1970!

No player's provided more Copa America assists in total than Argentina's Leo Messi! **12**

195+
No nation's played more Copa America matches than Uruguay!

5
Argentina and Uruguay have lost five Copa America penalty shootouts each – more than anyone else!

2

Two teams made their Gold Cup debut in 2019 – Bermuda and Guyana. Nice!

7

The 2012 AFCON top scorer prize was shared by seven players, including Pierre-Emerick Aubameyang. Wow!

STRANGE but true!

Cameroon at the AFCON

We can't get enough of strange footy kits, and one of the weirdest ones we can remember appeared at the 2002 Africa Cup Of Nations! **Cameroon** headed into the tourno as a big favourite and, to stand out even more, Puma decided to give them **sleeveless** shirts that looked more like something you'd find on a basketball court! No worries, though – The Indomitable Lions obviously liked them, as they went on to win their fourth title! FIFA didn't allow them to wear them at the World Cup that same year, as there wasn't any room for the FIFA logo, so they had to add black sleeves to the shirts!

Cameroon at the World Cup

FULL-TIME QUIZ

2:0

Test your knowledge on everything related to the second part of this records-packed book!

WORDSEARCH

Can you find the 20 mega nations in this massive grid?

Argentina	Belgium
Brazil	Cameroon
Croatia	Egypt
England	France
Germany	Holland

Italy	Mexico
Northern Ireland	Paraguay
Portugal	Republic Of Ireland
Scotland	USA
Uruguay	Wales

Y	L	H	Q	T	X	A	I	T	A	O	R	C	C	N	R	N	G	Q
U	R	U	G	U	A	Y	L	A	T	M	H	D	B	W	Z	O	N	D
W	T	T	A	S	W	Z	E	L	P	Y	I	I	L	U	V	R	D	N
N	W	T	H	J	H	X	E	Y	Y	U	S	S	L	M	S	T	C	M
M	X	A	Z	S	E	H	O	L	L	A	N	D	B	K	B	H	K	P
G	N	V	F	A	D	A	R	G	E	N	T	I	N	A	I	E	B	S
E	W	J	H	C	N	V	S	X	X	C	M	D	D	J	Q	R	E	B
F	R	V	S	C	A	J	Y	W	B	E	N	N	G	H	Z	N	S	A
U	E	W	S	B	L	E	N	D	R	A	K	U	P	M	H	I	U	U
K	P	R	V	B	T	T	M	G	L	G	B	W	H	O	H	R	K	G
J	U	U	L	H	O	G	J	G	B	Q	N	G	A	P	O	E	Y	Y
B	B	R	Z	R	C	S	N	H	B	Q	O	J	D	U	R	L	P	W
I	L	K	J	F	S	E	R	T	T	H	O	L	T	P	A	A	I	F
T	I	Z	C	G	U	Q	L	D	B	B	R	A	Q	W	A	N	H	E
F	C	S	G	Z	A	C	I	J	E	T	E	S	Z	L	V	D	V	G
D	O	O	D	U	P	C	M	O	L	H	M	U	C	G	S	Z	R	Y
X	F	B	G	T	G	D	W	P	G	W	A	L	V	D	T	R	N	P
D	I	C	D	I	E	B	T	H	I	U	C	Q	J	G	R	B	L	T
S	R	I	N	U	Q	L	C	D	U	L	R	B	W	C	R	B	I	O
K	E	U	L	Q	R	Y	P	O	M	F	X	U	Z	Y	P	V	Z	N
U	L	N	Z	J	C	M	Z	Q	B	F	O	T	U	O	B	B	A	L
O	A	E	D	Z	Q	U	P	Y	R	Y	G	D	R	R	T	G	R	N
C	N	R	V	F	L	Q	Z	A	S	H	B	T	Q	R	I	E	B	S
I	D	Z	Y	Z	G	C	N	A	N	S	U	N	F	A	B	R	B	E
X	L	Z	K	P	G	C	K	N	G	G	B	R	I	W	F	M	P	L
E	B	W	G	T	E	I	H	K	A	D	I	S	T	S	X	A	K	A
M	E	Y	V	I	U	X	J	L	F	Z	V	A	A	Z	Y	N	P	W
T	U	P	A	R	A	G	U	A	Y	Z	A	C	L	C	A	Y	X	T
G	T	C	L	Y	X	M	Z	Z	O	E	O	F	Y	C	S	N	G	Y

TRUE or FALSE?

Are these real or made up? Put a tick or cross in the box!

1 It took Brazil a whopping 28 years to bag their first ever World Cup trophy!

2 Superstar Cristiano Ronaldo has played in over 20 Euro Championship matches!

3 England have always played their home matches at national stadium Wembley!

4 Wales were a really impressive 15th in the FIFA World Rankings in April 2018!

5 No country's won more Copa America trophies in history than Uruguay!

6 The gigantic Rose Bowl Stadium can be found in the southern part of Mexico!

MATCH!

QUIZ ANSWERS!

HALF-TIME QUIZ

TRUE OR FALSE?
1. True;
2. False;
3. False;
4. False;
5. True;
6. False.

WHO AM I?
Paolo Maldini.

WORDFIT
See right.

MATCH THE FACTS!
1F; 2A; 3E; 4D; 5C; 6B.

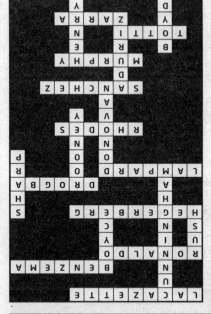

FULL-TIME QUIZ

TRUE OR FALSE?
1. True;
2. True;
3. False;
4. False;
5. True;
6. False.

WORDSEARCH
See right.